THE STORY DIGEST

ISBN # 978-0-6151-7511-9

FOR FRIENDS AND FAMILY
WITH LOVE.

TABLE OF CONTENTS

Chapter 1
Women Advice for Men
Helpful Insights

Chapter 2
Opinions about Religion
 & Religious Influence

Chapter 3
Opinions about American Attitudes
 & Society

Chapter 4
Marriage & Relationships
Includes: Want to see something funny?

Chapter 5
Communication Breakdown

Chapter 6
Understanding Truck Driving:
What every motorist needs to know.

Includes: Cruisin' with Susan: Accidents, Animals & Wonder Moments * Heroes of the Highway * Trucker Buddy Program * Best & Worst Roads for Driving, Designs, etc.. Best & Worst Drivers by City.

Chapter 7
Hollywood Info: Living & Working
in Hollywood
Includes: Celebrity Encounters; Chuck Norris, Robert Urich, Charlie Sheen, Dustin Hoffman, Kevin Bacon & More

Chapter 8
Writers & The Writing Life.
Includes over 50 Story Ideas

Chapter 9
Business Ideas: Two for you & me. Making Money

Chapter 10 The Years That Matter   Essay
Includes: Treading Through Molasses * Death Dream * The Crying Man * Letter From A Drug Abuser

Chapter 11 Moments in Youth   Short Stories
Includes: * Halloween Horrors * Little Sister's Revenge * Fish Story
* Bratty Little Sis * The Candy Bar * Poker Night at The Miller's
* Burnt Log * Queen of Skateboard Hill * Burnt Marshmallows * Bear Attack * Snake
Under Bed * The Hallway Incident * 1ˢᵗ Time Drunk * Fire Ext (high school) * Switzerland
'79' * Throw Me Into The Waves

Chapter 12   Recipes for you to enjoy!
Includes: English Chili * Singles Chili Mac Supreme * Lisa's Mom's Spinach Dip *
Rowan's Artichoke Dip * Linda's Garlic Chicken * John's Garlic Pork Chops *
Urich's Backyard Burgers * Paul's Hollywood Dish * Sooz Avacado Dip * Janette's
Wonderful Lasagna

Chapter 13 Ghost Encounters.
Includes: Ghost Moose, Who's Scratching my legs? I Dream of Fire, Ghostly Kiss, I'm out
of my Body, Stop Following Me!!

Chapter 14 Treasure Hunting in Florida Siesta Key, Key West, and St. Augustine.

CHAPTER 1
ADVICE FOR MEN ABOUT WOMEN

Do's & Don'ts. Ever wonder what went wrong? Why is she angry? What did you say or do? The first thing many men do when they speak to a women is insult her intelligence. Women do not like stupid men. Many men start out with obvious lies. Most women are only being polite. Inside, they are rolling their eyes and saying to themselves "another idiot". Don't make the mistake of thinking she believes you just Because she's being polite.

Quite a number of men often seem to have the same m.o.(method of operation). I have found that many women are not impressed by bad talk about an ex-spouse or ex-girlfriend. That kind of talk only makes the man look stupid. It is the feeling of many women I have spoken to that they agree, men need to be worthy of her time. Many, NOT ALL, men seem to feel they need to Be the authority on everything. Unfortunately, the use of "help" as a reason to approach a women has been frequently abused. Many women, I'd say most, cannot trust a man. We must be cautious at all times.

I would suggest, DO NOT ASSUME a women needs help, and never assume a women doesn't know anything. Rather, ask her, if there is anything you can help her with. You may wind up more often than not, insulting her ability to do the task, whatever the task she's doing at the time. This is where her self-esteem can be hurt. Unless, of course, she is a women that would rather someone do most things for them. It's up to her. But most women can do more than most men think they can. They are plenty capable.

And many men think they are innocently just trying to "help" her. That's where "don't assume she needs help" comes into play. You may find that many women become offended by unsolicited help. Some, NOT ALL, men seem to "push a women aside" and take over doing the task. Just to show her he can do it. This is an offensive gesture. It's not noble, and it's not help. Unless she asks for help, it's best to leave her alone. And whatever you do, NEVER stand around watching her and "supervising". You'll piss her off. She is more than capable and competent to do the job.

Only men that are secure in themselves will not bother a women when she's working. Nor will they be offended or insulted if she doesn't need his help.
The in-secure macho guys are the one's that feel the need to "take charge" and fake like they know everything. Macho guys don't make a good impression.

Many, NOT ALL, men use the word "Independent" as a way to dismiss a women, and what is important to her. They say "Oh, she's just independent, she doesn't need any help". Many women are independent. Meaning they are capable and competent to take care of themselves. Many women do not need a man to "take care" of her in the meaning of the old, traditional way.

With more and more opportunities for women in America, many choose to stay single, attend college, work, or have a career rather than go into motherhood right away. And just because she may be dating or living with a man, doesn't mean he needs to "take care" of her.

It doesn't mean he's "in charge" of her life. He has no right to try and control her. I am aware that it works both ways. Too much nagging at your spouse gets you gone. I think too many people have a "ownership" mentality when it comes to relationships.

We don't and never will "own" another person. That way only upsets the natural balance. Work together, not against each other. Those that are secure in themselves will have a much easier time in a relationship. If, for some reason, you are a in-secure person, perhaps some counseling is needed to help sort out what you feel and why you're feeling that way.

There is no shame in seeking counseling. It's the logical and practical solution to some problems you may have. No-one should be made to feel guilty about it. Perhaps, that could be part of your problem.…..(those that are in your daily life, i.e., home, family, work, etc..) playing guilt trips on you. Putting pressure on you to live your life how they want, etc.

What training courses are there available at a young age to teach us about relationships and dating?? I don't know of any, do you? In some schools, they teach social studies. But I don't remember anything about human behavior, etiquette, understanding each other, and so on. Now, there are numerous books on these subjects available in book stores, but not in classrooms, as far as I know. I think human relationships are a good and necessary subject, and it couldn't hurt to include such teachings in public schools throughout America.

Perhaps they should make a "video" game about how to catch and keep a women. In the game, you have to say and do all the right things, and mean it. For real. Otherwise you lose and have to start over. This may be a good training tool in male/female relationships. Although, not all relationships are plain cut and dry.

They do get complicated. But communication is key to sorting out any misunderstandings or confusions. Maybe we can help some of our children, and, maybe even help ourselves understand this murky confusion trial and error fighting and loving thing we call relationships. After all, we are drawn together by natural instinct and need. Sure, sex is easy, not much thought needed there. But everything else!!! Fighting, controlling, nagging, cheating, assuming, jealousy, anger, confusion, and on and on. We're a nation of control freaks!!

Another thing that can get a women upset, frustrated or flabbergasted. Is when a man doesn't know what he did wrong? He's completely clueless!! Men, here is some help for you: Don't push your "help" on her. Don't question or doubt her. Don't assume. Don't try to be the authority on everything. Instead of trying to understand women, rather, just try to understand logic. An example is: When a women has her monthly menstrual cycle, some men make stupid comments about that natural biological event. There is nothing new or wrong with a women's period. It's just biology. But some people have to make something stupid out of what comes natural. It's just logic to accept it as it is.

And don't say anything stupid with regards to it. It's just a natural part of life!! Same as a man's daily masturbating. Just a natural thing. No big deal. Women, you can't live with them, and you can't live without them, and…..you can't control or own them. And you have no right to assume you own them. We must un-learn most of what we were raised on, or so it seems. It clashes with the free country and free attitude we live in. The religious tradition may try to make their followers live that way, by the bible, say. But outside, in the real world, freedom prevails. It's the way most people choose to live. Both worlds collide.

The bible says one thing, and freedom says another. Which side are you on? Which way do you choose to live? And then find a companion that lives the same way. Free people will not be bound by the bible or any religious way. It's a whole different life and mentality. So we can't expect people to obey and allow the man to control the household and the women to serve him. In the free world, it doesn't, and will not ever, work that way. In the free world, there is a balance in the household that is expected. Not a one-way, my way or the highway, way of life. Those two worlds collide and we may not even be so aware of why we are clashing in the home so often.

It's freedom verses the restrictions and rules of religion or subconsciously religious influences. Once we understand where our problems and attitudes come from, can we begin to understand where we are in the larger scheme of things. Live and plan our lives better. We spend too much time fighting, clashing, not understanding, trying to control each other, and not understanding why we believe or behave in this way or that way.

I have some theories regarding problems between men and women. Many of us were raised a certain way. Mostly with some kind of religious influence. And then when we become adults we run free from everything that binds us. Rules, religion, parents, school, etc.. And we begin to live our lives how we want. Which often clashes with how we were raised. Because as we get older, we begin to think for ourselves and form our own opinions.

But some things stick with us. And we can be confused or mislead into thinking we must live this way or that. But in reality, the people you meet do not subscribe to the same beliefs. Perhaps, when we meet, we should lay out our feelings and beliefs up front. So we know more of what we are getting ourselves into. Example: If you are a man and expect a women to obey you and you expect to be completely in charge of the household, based on how you were raised, what you've been told and taught up to this point, and some possible religious influence. And you meet a women that is often described as "Independent", and does not subscribe to the same way of life…..There you have it. No match.

She will not allow you to control her. Men should never expect a women to follow that way of life. Unless you both have an understanding ahead of time. You sit down and have a discussion about your views and feelings. Just because it may be what you were taught, how you were raised, etc… does not mean women today will follow. We women have spent centuries fighting for our fair and equal treatment, and freedom. We, our generations of women, are not going to give up what we have fought for and won. Yes, we are Independent.

Yes, we are capable and competent. Yes, we want a relationship with a man, but not a relationship with a macho, insecure, control freak that has been mislead in his life. He was not taught more information that he needed to know. So now he's an adult, running around and trying to hook up with women. And since he was not given all the info he needs, he becomes a problem and a waste of time to most of the women he encounters. And he is angry, frustrated and most likely confused. He damns women. He cannot seem to understand them.

He can't seem to say or do anything right. It's because he was not given the important information he needed to know before he got old enough to chase women.
Whatever he was taught and told, is backfiring on him now. It's not even close to working in the world that he lives and works in today. This day and age.

It is the common belief that men that behave macho, are really weak and afraid. This is what the macho behavior suggests. These type of men then expect women to give up certain aspects of her life for him? This macho attitude can on some instances cause men to do stupid things. Examples: putting a dog in the back of his pickup truck and not tying the dog down. So the dog winds up falling or jumping out of the bed and being killed.

Or, putting things in the pickup bed and not covering them for rain and tying them down properly. And even leaving the tailgate open, so the items then fall out. All because he feels he needs to be in charge and when the women points out these minor mistakes, he stubbornly ignores her and then winds up losing some or all of the items. And this only makes the guy look extremely stupid.

It doesn't matter how big or small the incidents are, it's what happens and why, that is important to understand. Some, NOT ALL, men feel a power struggle. He may feel he needs to be the boss and the women to follow his lead. But, today's women, free, intelligent, and independent will, in most cases, not follow.

Because macho behavior by men is not at all desirable to women. Most women do not like stupid, insecure, macho men. They are looking for a good balance. Not someone to be in charge and then do one dumb macho thing after another. This type of man is not qualified to be in charge.

He needs to relax, listen to her, and work together as a team. Some, NOT ALL, men feel that working with a women in this way is a sign of weakness. Women don't see it that way. Women see it as intelligent. Smart. And not a power struggle, constant clashing.
Most women will not allow an insecure, incompetent man to be in charge of her life. That's just the way it is. And when some men treat a women badly by condescending her, he won't last very long.

Women will not stick around for it. That kind of man is just a waste of her time, frustrating, and not enjoyable at all to be around. Condescending: questioning and doubting her. Asking stupid questions instead of trying to think. Think logically. And….reading a map or asking for directions on a road trip, is a sign of intelligence. Not doing so is macho, stupid, and weak. And a man's macho behavior is one reason women argue a lot of the time.

If you consider yourself an intelligent man, then prove it. SHOW HER. By working *with* her, not against her. There is no need to be fearful that you will look weak to her. Who told you that? I think this attitude is taught to men, by men. Maybe men teach this to sabotage his competition. So the guy screws up with this chick, and now they break up, and now the other guy can go for the women in question. Or men just put this kind of macho pressure on each other. Who really knows?

But, know this: women know a smart, dumb, or weak man when she sees him. Don't allow what other men have told you to influence how you deal with women. They may be misleading. Like the blind leading the blind!!! And most women out there have to deal with this……daily!! A note about teasing and joking: Don't joke "about" her, "to" her. It's not going to be funny. You can joke about anything or anyone else, just don't tease her or joke about her. You may come off sounding insulting.

It's not that women are sensitive, it's that women get hassled a lot, mistreated, condescended and so on. Most women have to fight and put up with a lot of crap in their daily lives. Most of that crap comes from men trying to dominate them. So women fight back. And fight for respect and independence. Also, it has been experienced by many women that some, NOT ALL, men seem to NOT be able to handle it when a women knows anything. Or when a women speaks up and points out a suggestion or obvious mistake. Some, NOT ALL, men react by dismissing her knowledge or suggestion. Basically ignoring her as though she is not in the room.

I think this may have something to do with being competitive. He has his eyes on the prize and she is a threat to him. So he pushes her aside, so to speak. Well, as many men have experienced, most women will not be pushed aside or ignored. They can and will find a different route to the same solution. They will just work around the obstacle in their way. And I know this can infuriate some men. I say again, work together, not against. Don't upset the natural balance. And you both can prosper. If you don't want to work together, perhaps a different working venue is more suitable for you. You can work on your own. Without any female interference. But, being that most work places are equal opportunity, like women have fought for and won over the centuries, means that working together is the protocol. Like it or not. Like it, or leave.

Contrary to popular belief (or so it seems), so called "fat ugly" women ARE NOT easy. Who told you this? All women, regardless of how they look, deserve respect. And these women aren't stupid either. They know b.s. when they see it. No matter the situation. If all you are after is sex, lying will only get you fights and headaches, and I'm sure it's not worth it. As far as most women are concerned, you lie, you deserve the hell you get for it.

Try being more honest. Try "I'm not interested in a relationship, just interested in a little sex". Many men are afraid this approach won't work. They think they have to lie and be cunning and sneaky to get sex. The "direct" approach certainly can't work, he thinks. But, have you tried it? There are women out there that may want to hook up with you. Or maybe not. Maybe she doesn't want the headache of a relationship either. But to lie and mislead her into thinking you are going to stick with her, be a good friend and companion, and then 3 months later turn into a jerk just to get rid of her........well. You'll have hell to pay for lying and trickery.

And don't use the "m" word (marriage) on her either. Just to get her in the sack. That trick won't work either, guys. I am fully aware that this goes both ways. And men can, and I'm sure have, written their own books from their own perspective and experiences. Many men have referred to women as "bitches". And there's nothing like lying to a women to really bring out the bitch in her. If you don't like a bitch, don't put yourself in that situation in the first place!!

RESPECT: Has to be earned. It's not just automatically given. Some people are forceful and aggressive and may believe that they are being respected. Or they behave that way because they feel that is the only way to get respect. But, what they don't realize is that many people around them, in their daily lives, do not respect them. And will not. They are only going along with an act. It could be out of fear of bodily harm, or just trying to keep the peace. But a forceful and overly aggressive person will never be respected.

Only tolerated. And only for a short time. We all should know that it's considered rude to stare at people. Some women have an uncomfortable, creepy feeling when we notice a man staring at us. Look, but don't get caught staring. There may be some men out there that may think a women to be stuck up, too snooty to be friendly to him. But, it's possible, if he's staring at her a lot, that she can sense it and is feeling uneasy. She will move fast to get out of his eyesight. This is another reason that girls and women travel in packs. For safety and protection. We are aware of the predators around us. And PLEASE, flush the toilet after using it. Practice cleanliness and good hygiene. You will impress a women more by being clean. Women *do not* want to be your mother.

As for many girls & women, there doesn't seem to be anything special left for them, with regards to men. It has been destroyed, trampled on, shredded. Many girls and women find that being friends with a gay man or men is very rewarding and enjoyable. They seem to be more fun to hang around, and obviously not threatening or insulting to women. What do gay men have that straight men don't?

1. Gay men do not insult women's intelligence.
2. Subtract the stupid macho guy and you have someone that's more secure in themselves and more fun to be around.
3. Gay men seem to be more secure in themselves, and a lot happier than straight men.
4. Gay men do not carry the same straight white man's burden.
5. Straight women do not have to worry about sex when they are around gay men.

6. Gay men can be strong and protective of women, in a cute, non-insulting big brother kind of way.

7. There is less domestic violence with gay men. Sure, they can and have fought with each other, but for the most part, and the gay community at whole, there is far less domestic violence.

8. Gay men have a sensibility and sensitivity that far too many straight men do not posses.

9. Gay men are A LOT cleaner than many straight men. Their homes, and especially bathrooms are very sanitary and fashionably impressive.

Gay men flush after toilet use!! And they wash their hands!! And they cook, and are very sweet natured and happy.

10. Gay men are not threatened or intimidated by straight women. They generally get along just fine with women.

Many, NOT ALL, men try to destroy a women's ambitions. For reasons of sex, power & control. They get in a women's way, when she tries to accomplish something in her life. College education, buying a home or land, travel, and other things. These type of men try to break a women down. Keep her down. Make her weak and dependent on him. And they go as far as abuse everything that most girls and women naturally hold dear. Like the hope and/or idea of marriage.

Some, NOT ALL, men even abuse *this*. They throw out the "m" word just to pull her in and try to score with her. They tell a women what he thinks she wants to hear. Women cannot trust men. We cannot risk our hearts and minds to the abuse and lies of some, NOT ALL, men. And of course, we cannot risk our bodies, and spirits as well. Women have to be more and more protective of ourselves and each other. As mentioned before, there is not much left that was once "special" to girls and women, that has not been violated, and shattered by the lies, power, control, and abuse by some, NOT ALL, but enough to have done significant damage, men.

In closing;

GUYS: Good luck out there. Remember, don't lie, don't assume, don't try to be the authority on everything, don't abuse "help". And so on. Be honest, and secure in yourself. Don't be afraid or intimidated. Don't let anyone push you around or mislead you. To be a man, a real man, is to be honorable, respectful, caring, and decent. Women have fought for freedom, equal treatment, respect, and independence. Work together, not against. Be smart. You CAN do it. You CAN improve your chances and relationships with women. You CAN understand women and live in peace and harmony together.

CHAPTER 2
OPINIONS ABOUT RELIGION & RELIGIOUS INFLUENCE

I for one don't appreciate it when religious people shove their beliefs on me. Religion is a
option. Not to be forced on a free individual. Guilt trips to try and scare people into
following their way. It is my opinion that they try to control people by fear. It's another way
of gaining power and control over people.

Some weak, some easy to manipulate, to brainwash. I don't doubt there may have been Jesus
at one time. But what scientific proof do we have he's coming back? What physical evidence
is there? There are so many biblical scholars that disagree over the history. There are so
many religions, do we wonder why? They all say theirs is the true way. How many people
can resist the allure of power? If some or all aspects of the religion you choose, or have been
born into, work well for you. Enhance your life in a good, harmless, meaningful way, good
for you. But if the religion brainwashes it's people into carrying out threats, or death, free
people will always fight it.

To be made to feel guilty by family, for choosing not to follow, I believe, is wrong. We live
in a free county, but often when we choose to live our own way, we are condemned by
religious influence on society. We don't seem to separate religion and society. You see how
much power and control the religion already has over many people? Even in our own
families, we often have to live a lie. Just go along with the motions to appease them. Yeah,
sure. Freedom means not having to fight to live free when you already are born and raised in
a free county like ours--America. You are allowed to practice your religion without fear of
our government.

We people that choose no religion at all, should also be allowed to live without
condemnation, or harassment from our families. *You* believe Jesus is the only way? I believe
he is merely an option. So many followers think he's going to come back. He was placed in
his tomb, it took many men to roll the boulder and seal the tomb. It took just as many men
to roll the boulder, open the tomb, and take Jesus's body. Strong people can be very
manipulating and convincing. So many people believed. Maybe it made their lives easier. It
was their choice to believe and follow. Their option. Jesus is the way for *some* people, NOT
ALL. Free thinkers, live free.

CHAPTER 3
OPINIONS ABOUT AMERICAN
ATTITUDES AND SOCIETY

Includes: Workplace harassment *
Influence of movies, tv, religion, bullies * basic manners, smoking, and everyday behavior.

We have a lot in common. We're American. Born. Raised. Long family history. Pride.
American flags on our homes and cars. We work our butts off. Pay Taxes! (well, most of us
do). Baseball, football, freedom. We love it and we are so very lucky to be here. In this
country. HELL YEAH!! One of our favorite pastimes is to bitch and complain. Get up on
our soap boxes and talk to whoever wants to listen. To argue. To debate. 1st Amendment.
Yeah! We are so much alike. And some of us are alike in our double lives.

We look one way on the outside. Nice, clean, normal, happy family, nice house, car, kids,
dog. We all know too well some deception. Lies. Cheating. Back-stabbing. Crime. Drugs.
That hurt and destroy so many of us common Americans. Condemnation for those that
don't " fit in". Fear. Fear of the unknown. People that are different from them. What would
your friends, family, coworkers, and neighbors think of you? Some, obviously NOT ALL,
can be so quick to attack our fellow Americans. Gossip. Discrimination. Violence.
Destruction of property.

We lack discipline. Some people are so afraid to be kind. To care. Where did this idea, or
action come from? My opinion: Religion. The centuries of power and control that have had,
and some still have, over many Americans. Conform or be cast-out. Some people rather
choose to be outcasts. It's more free out there. They live life their own way in their own
micro-society. All the while working, paying bills, mortgages, taxes, and not committing
crimes against their fellow man or women.

They are clean, decent, kind, caring folks, that don't "fit-in" with what is considered by many
to be "main-stream". I have noticed, to my pleasure, over the past years that "main-stream"
has dissolved considerably. Less religious pressure. Less society pressure. Less, but still there,
stress. More and more generations have been "breaking free" of our parents society of
restrictive, guilt ridden, loaded down with stress, way of life. We don't buy into it. We do our
own thing. And we are changing the way we raise our children. Finding out more and more
through our own feelings and beliefs, which direction we want to live and take our children
with us.

More freedom. That's the bottom line.

I feel that too many people in our society push people into fear. Which causes the reaction of smoking cigarettes, dope, excessive alcohol consumption, abusing drugs, etc.. Our society pushes some people into this abusive behavior. The pressure to "fit in", to keep our parents and family happy. Do what "they" want you to do. They put fear in your hearts and minds starting at a early age, and continuing your whole life. Some people put way too much importance on material things. Having the latest car, stereo, clothes, styles, etc.. The "fit in" mentality.

Competitiveness. Controls them like puppets. When asked why they do these things, the answer usually is "to fit-in". "To be cool". The attitude we have of what's cool needs to obviously change. It should be "cool" NOT to do stupid and weak things. It should be cool to stand up for yourself and not let anyone talk you into doing something wrong, illegal, or stupid. People do these things because they are afraid and weak.

When we are growing up and see our heroes, regardless if they are comic book, fiction, or movies and tv, they are still our heroes. We look up to them, right? Did any of your heroes do something stupid? Did they smoke cigarettes, do drugs, abuse alcohol?? ABSOLUTELY NOT!! Is Batman and Spiderman wimpy? Weak? Stupid? So then why should we live our lives like that? What are our everyday adversaries?? Our parents? Yes. It can be true. And some parents aren't going to like this, but too bad. Our families? The punks at school? The asshole boss or co-workers at work? So, I ask you, are these people so big and bad that you can't stand up to them? And are they so powerful that you can't turn your back on what harms you and be strong? Are you a wimp? Are you weak? Are you stupid?

I'm sure you don't think of yourself in any of these negative ways. So why act like it then? Stand up to your adversaries. Be your own super hero. Don't let anyone push you around. Don't let them make you feel bad for wanting to live your life your way, and do the right things. Things that are right in life. Right with the natural spiritual balance of nature. And right with the law. We have laws for a reason. Do you like it if someone does something bad to you? No, of course not. Then why do something bad to them? You're only sabotaging yourself. Holding your life back from your dreams and full potential. Some folks have laughed at me because I don't have much. No nice home, nice car, nice clothes, jewelry, etc.. But I don't fight to have those things. I don't steal to have them. I'm not competitive.

I am happy with the small and simple life I have. I say to them, " I may not have much, but I don't have too much debt, and I don't have to worry about the law". I live more freely this way. But it is my way. And not always suitable for other people. But we can sometimes obsess about having all the nicest material things. And we can work hard and enjoy them. But I would not want to carry so much weight on my shoulders. That's my choice. I'm a simpleton. Imagine a society in where people are not motivated by greed, money, big homes, big cars, big status, and so on.

Look at many of our movies and tv shows. What do they really have to work with? What do they have in common? It's "what motivates people in general". We see it too much every day. If we put such high importance on these say, finer things, or bigger things, then we are allowing ourselves to be pushed. Yes, I agree having goals to work for and achieve are rightful and noble things. And living good off the rewards of your honest labor is perfectly acceptable. But for those of us that do not make hoards of money every year, this is where it gets interesting? Messy?

We have seen shows and read books where the main character *isn't* motivated or driven by greed, money, etc.. And he is a noble character. Many people like to see people like that. Now, to live like that is another thing. If someone says to you "Let's go rob a store, get cash and buy the latest in cool clothing, and have enough left over to get drugs and drunk and party. C'mon, whatya say?". Now, think about it. This guy is putting importance on these items: money, fancy clothes, drugs, alcohol, excitement of doing a stupid crime.

Now, let's say you're the kind of person that would rather *not* live your life like that. You do not put so much importance on these things. You are not motivated by the same things that your friend is. You, I say, are more free. And smarter. You are not being played like a stupid puppet. You think for yourself. You are your own super hero. You say no thanks, and walk away. You have no fear. No fear of that friend or his buddies. No fear of ridicule. Because you don't think these material things are that important. You have a bounce in your step because you have less weight on your shoulders and in your heart. You are more free than your friend and his buddies are.

Calling people on their fear can have a profound effect. But be very careful with this, you can wind up getting your butt kicked. Calling them on their fear has a way of disarming them in a way. Now that you know their little "secret", and they KNOW that you know. You have exposed something deeply private and personal to them. Like taking a stab in the dark and hitting your mark "dead-on". It can sometimes, have the effect of taking some of the wind out of their sails so to speak. It lightens them. They begin to calm down a little. Now that they cannot hide behind it anymore, that they are "exposed" now, they react in a funny kind of way. You'll see it.

A significant reaction. Some may respond by trying to be big and tough and deny it. Deny that they have been hiding behind this barrier of fear for so long. Calling them on it. They smoke cigarettes because they were weak and wanted to "fit-in". Now they stink and look like a fool, not cool. And everyone else around them has to choke on their nasty habit. They advertise their weakness by smoking, drugs, alcohol abuse, etc.. And here they are trying to act like everything's fine. And they are tough and not afraid of anyone or anything. But it's the fear that causes these substance abuses. The drugs and alcohol are their crutches, that hold them up. Why is it that doing something stupid is considered cool? It should be the other way around. People are too weak to stand up to the peer pressure.

They have been beaten down so much. By the weight of it all. Of "it", I refer to life in general, stress, pressures, fears. They collapse under the weight. They can't handle it, or so they have convinced themselves. In some cases, their families have encouraged this weakness. Have "enabled" it. Ah, the things we do to each other. The hurt and pain we dish out. How can we continue to live like this? We should know better. We should care enough not to hurt each other. We are better than that. This is not civilization as it *can* be.

We all possess the power to control our own behavior towards each other. We cannot control what happens to us, but we can control how we react to what happens to us. CREDIT CARD DEBT: Do you realize you can be in debt your entire adult life? And here we are actually thinking that "It'll all be paid off before retirement age". Yeah, right. We have been fooling ourselves too long!!! Too much greed. Too much "gotta have it now" mentality. Too many suckers are born every day, and they stay that way their whole lives.

Thinking to themselves "It's only a little debt". Now, obviously buying a home, land, decent car are important. Emergencies are important too. Buying new shoes is not a emergency. Again, I say, we put too much importance on "having the latest, and having it NOW". The credit card companies love you. They want you to be stupid and weak. They want you to be buried in debt and live way beyond your means. After all, you just absolutely have to have it all. And have it all right this very minute. What's the problem here? Why do we need to have it all NOW!!? Are we trying to impress each other? Are we trying to "fit-in". Have the right look, etc..? Ok, enough already.

We need to fall back. Back off the debt thing. Save up and pay cash for it. If you can't pay cash for it, then maybe you shouldn't have it? Except, obviously, if it's a house, land, car, emergency, etc.. Do you really want to be in debt every single day of your entire adult life??? Do you want to die in debt? How many pairs of shoes can you wear? How many cars can you drive? How many TV's can you watch? Clothes can you wear?

Etc.., etc… blah, blah. Isn't it just a teeensie bit overwhelming? Ok, stop already. Enough. Put the brakes on it. Can it. For crying out loud! No more un-important debt ok? We need discipline. With so many aspects of our lives. Some of us. Not all. Some people are doing just fine. Some though, need discipline with behavior at work, attitude, spending, lying, cheating, crime, every day rights and wrongs. Fighting with each other. Hurting each other.

Letting our insecurities get the best of us. Letting that fear control our behavior. Letting the fear determine how bad we treat each other. There is always something behind that jerk we deal with. It starts there. With the instigator. And his/her fears. Do or say something stupid, it's the fear. The fear has gotten to them. That's why they act like that. The bad habit many of us have in calling a young person "kid" can be interpreted as an insult. Someone older just throwing around their superiority. Age superiority.

I think it's disrespectful to teens and young adults to call them "kids". With the advent of the internet and home computers these days, young people are no longer kept "in the dark" so to speak. Like days of old. Especially young girls and women. I feel that society has tried mightily to hold them back by not allowing them vital information they need to know, to protect themselves in every day situations, and to get ahead in life.

I know of many women, myself included, that have felt angry and frustrated at this interference. We no longer have to ask people that would only give us a reply "you're too young", or "you're a girl. Girl's aren't supposed to do those things, or know certain things". Now we have computers and the internet and get all the info we need. And can become even more self-confident and knowledgeable than ever.

I believe in preparing our young people possibly sooner than tradition has in the past. Keeping them innocent and naïve for too long. By the time they get out of high school, they still do not know many important things they need to, in order to be ready when situations arise. Certain words, terms, actions, drugs, mistrust, etc.. Throwing them into the world and it's "sink or swim?".

It has been a tradition to gasp in horror at the mention of teaching young people about sex and real life, when they are young. It is forbidden. You don't say those things around little innocents ears. Even when little innocent is curious and is asking about it. To further his/her knowledge and experience. Children do see and hear everything around them. And they take it all in. They listen. And I'm certain they understand a lot more than we may realize. They think logically. It's part of the survival instinct. Stronger and more heightened instinct at a younger age. They witness events around them and come to logical conclusions.

They may figure, what they see is the direction their lives will take when they get older. Sex, Marriage, Kids, that's how it's done. Or….in a unstable household, God only knows what these children see and hear, and what they learn may seem right and normal to them. I think our public schools should cover many more bases of vital information that sadly, many homes and parents do not. Either some parents avoid it all together, which harms the child's development. Or the parents themselves were never taught discipline, basic manners, respect for others, including themselves, work ethics, and so on. Our public schools can step in and make sure the children are covered on important topics.

Usually reserved for learning in the home. We can see as a result of non-learning, what type of adults these children become. You see the crime, and behavior problems of some people in the workplace, or dating, marriage, relationships, and so on. These adults grew up to be problems to a educated, disciplined, civilized society. They were simply not taught what they need to know to ease into working relationships with other individuals. What most of us learn as peaceful, balanced, hard working, respectful, lifestyles.

Our society needs to change it's attitudes about supposed failure. For the people that haven't changed already. For the most part. I feel that the attitude of failure is a influence of religion. Live our way or you'll be a failure. To be made to feel guilty. I see failure as a learning tool, a stepping stone to future success. It's a measuring device. In life's learning process. Some people say that young people will "fail" if they get married and have children too young. I really wonder what kind of attitude and support system do we have in place to allow the young people (by young, I mean 18 and over, legal adults), to live how they choose.

We seem to feel that having a child is bad. It's wrong. It's nothing but a big mistake. Do you realize the emotional stress and pressure that puts on the young people? Yes, having a family should be planned for optimum success. But we do not live our lives strictly following orders and a life must do list. We follow our hearts, and our emotions. And…our hormones. We obviously need to prepare and be responsible, that is obvious. But, if the 18 and over young people are legally allowed to marry and have children, then why do they get hassled and yelled at and condemned, and made to feel bad for following their hearts.

We make this world tough for ourselves and our young people. How can they support themselves and the baby we say? There are systems in place to assist them when they need it. And some young people are responsible enough to get work and take care of their family. Ever notice how grandparents reminisce about their past? How "in-love" they were and oh how young they were? He was in the military, and she was pregnant with their first child? Is it an American tradition to struggle with the basic human need of having love and a family when we are young?

We say it's supposed to be easier when we're older. We are making more money. We are more mature, etc.. But we are also older, more tired, more set in our ways, more spoiled by our freedoms, etc.. What is best for the baby? To be in a loving environment, where they are welcomed into this world with love and acceptance. Not…oh, you've given birth to a lifelong mistake. The baby is a burden. You're too young.

You can't even take care of yourself!! And on goes the attack of negativity. It doesn't take long for depression to set in and destroy this young family before they can barely get started. They are made to feel bad because that is what SOCIETY and Religion are telling them. Having your basic needs like a modest home, and the best job you can get, working together, and it will work out just fine. I think young people aren't that stupid and naïve. They will scramble and figure it out. And some do plan.

They are not afraid of plunging in and making it work. And work hard they will. For one thing, they want to prove all the negative people wrong. And that the young people will do just fine, especially if you leave them alone and stop telling them that they have made a big mistake, and they will do nothing but fail. I don't see having a family as a failure. I see it as a strength. A future. A loving and supportive family. I think some of us may let our fears get the best of us.

And some of us get out of control and do nothing but hassle the young people about their situation. If they are 18 and older, they are legally allowed to marry and have children. Maybe instead of making them feel bad because of our own fears, we should perhaps wish them well, relax, and calm down, and feel confident that the young couple will work things out.

They will work together. It's all part of the survival instinct. It will kick in and they'll hustle. And they can and will prove people wrong. After all, many of us were young once. And mistakes are not failures, just part of the learning process. And I feel we should not come down hard on our young people. Time will pass, and people will calm down, and things will be proven.

And people will get used to the new child and life will move on. And the world will once again be back in balance. A beautiful child is born, that is not a mistake or a failure. And that child should be in a loving home, with a loving and supportive family. We can all stop freaking out now, ok? Society may change, but the human body has not. We reach the age of human reproduction.

The whole reason for this is to carry on our species. But, we are also very complicated and often stupid creatures. We make far too much hassle and trouble where there does not need to be. We should be more peaceful, humble, and behave more intelligently, and spiritually when anything new arises in our lives. As most of us do, but many of us do not. I think too many of us carry too much stress from society and religious influence on our shoulders. Which can cause us to freak out, and lose control. Things do not have to be that way. We can be a lot more calmer than we are. If we choose to be.

For those that already live more peacefully and calm, I bet you feel a lot less stress. As for the others…It's nothing to be afraid of. We all need less stress. I think so many people may not believe enough in themselves that they can overcome anything that comes into their lives. I also think it's best to not pile too much on ourselves.

Again I re-iterate: putting too much importance and weight on what society and religion tells us to do, feel, and think. We can lift so much off our shoulders if we try. Life is not fair, but there's always a way to work around that. Don't give negativity that much power or weight. Or it may try to crush your spirits. And you cannot allow that in your life. I have some thoughts about movies and television. What I'm thinking about is really a subtle thing. I don't think many people may even realize it. But….we do pick things up subconsciously without even thinking about it. It becomes a part of us. Part of our every day behavior.

Most people know that most movies and television are fiction. Written from the imagination of writers. Thinking up all sorts of stories and situations to put the characters through. Well, part of that process is a common thing in Hollywood called "following the pattern". A movie will start out a bit slow, letting the audience get to know the characters. And then it begins to build. The plot thickens. The characters are in a tight spot and must get themselves out of it.

Then there is the big climax, the big confrontation between good and evil, and good wins, in the last 10 minutes of the movie. Wow, you say. Blown away by this fantastic movie going experience. It's a pattern. Designed to move the story along and keep the audiences short attention span interested. And one very big thing, common thing I notice in many films and television, is the fighting between the characters. The writers often put these fights in to make an obstacle for the hero to have to get around, or through. A favorite example of mine is: Man wants to quit his job and try his luck at pro golf. Wife, by some film law, must give him a hard time about it. Create a loud, yelling, bitchy, temper tantrum fight so he'll have to get through it.

Albeit tired, and exhausted. Both he and the audience. Now our hero grabs his golf bag and heads out the door. The story must pick up from there, and be a little lighter. To balance it out. Peaks and valleys. Then later, they kiss and make up, especially since he won mega bucks playing golf and now she believes in him, and can buy herself all the fancy shoes she wants. And so on.

What my point is, is this: Arguing for argument sake. It's a REALLY BAD habit we've picked up. And where did we get this idea to instantly jump into a fight or argument whenever he/she wants to do something? Subconsciously from movies and television. And possibly our parents as well. But where did they get it from? I just want you all to think about it, that's all.

I'd like to ask all Hollywood writers, please stop writing scenes like that? Try something more original. Thank you. I find it pretty surprising that people actually get shocked over certain things in life. Like people having affairs. Some people getting married, or divorced, or pregnant, or anything else in life that is just the regular, everyday, cycle of life. Some people act so surprised when they "hear the news". They act all high drama about it. Get all gossipy and excited. I think that's funny. What has happened, whatever it may be, is nothing at all new. It's just natural life happening as it will! And getting upset over something as natural as pimples, gray hair, and weight gain I think is silly.

You notice how easily people "freak out" about these things? Silly. I think we ought to start a trend in America. It's called the "AF" bars and clubs. AF for Alcohol Free. I know we have coffee shops, and they are nice, warm and cozy places to meet and have fun. And I'm well aware that every bar and club out there can serve non-alcoholic drinks. But what I'm after, is a completely alcohol free bar and club. With the same crowds, music, dancing, bands, food, and atmosphere. But without any and all alcohol. An "AF" bar and club. I think of this because I wonder what all we have out there to choose from?

Just about every bar or club I see, serves alcohol. It's always there, and in our faces. It's an option, I'm aware of that. But it's also an excepted attitude that when we go out to a bar or nightclub, we will drink some alcohol. Which, of course, can lead to all sorts of problems and troubles. I think we should be big and bold and have this "other" place we can go, and feel a lot lighter and cleaner, than getting drunk, vomiting all over the place, feeling sick and hung over the next day. And of course, drinking and driving, and getting into fights, etc.. If there are more "AF" bars and clubs around, people would still be able to have so much fun, and not with the hassles of alcohol. What do you think? Let's go to a "AF" bar or club tonight. Whatya say?

Some basic manners and etiquette: CLEAN UP AFTER YOURSELF IN PUBLIC BATHROOMS!! I know you don't want to get anything messy on your hands, but please, grab the mouse by the tail and place that thing in the proper disposal box that is ever present inside the women's restroom stall. Don't just dump it in the toilet. You wind up clogging up the toilet because you don't want to get your hands messy. Please, flush as many times as you need to get the toilet clean…for crying out loud!! And if you need to flush several times "during" your (ahem) activity, do so please . So you don't put 4 hand fulls of toilet paper in at one time, and clog it all up!!! FLUSH, FLUSH, FLUSH!!

If you don't want to sit on the toilet seat, don't just hover and pee all over it! Use the ass gaskets provided, or bring your own cleaning wipes to sanitize the seat before using it. For people that leave a mess, we shouldn't allow them to use these bathrooms. They can just go out back in the woods, hover and spray all they want. And they don't even have to flush! How about that? Just make sure to watch out for snakes!

I have an idea of why some men don't flush the toilet after using it. It's because ever since they were little boys, in a public bathroom, that has no privacy for them whatsoever, and they were doing their business, other boys would look over and check out their privates. How embarrassing is that? How uncomfortable does that make you feel? Being right out in the open for anyone to see your male parts?? No wonder they just zip up and bolt out of there as fast as they can. I think all public men's rooms should have privacy for them. So nobody can look at their goods while they are relieving themselves.

If there are some men's bathrooms that have privacy, good. But I think that's probably why they don't put the seat down at home, or hardly ever flush, and may hardly ever even wash up after touching themselves. Only they know how clean they are down there. There are some men that do not clean up after sex. They are disgusting!! Nasty, crusty, scumbags!! They don't wash!!

And then they want to shake your hand!!!??? Have you ever noticed after you shake someone's hand that if you smell your hand afterwards, you can smell the soap they used to wash up? Or….if you don't smell soap. What do you smell? Hey, don't be staring at other men's privates in a public bathroom!! Don't be a weirdo. And FLUSH!!! And wash your hands thoroughly. Thank you. Please, do not smoke cigarettes indoors. Please don't make the people around you have to choke on your smoke. And when in a laundry room, especially don't smoke in there either. Someone having just cleaned their clothes, all smelling nice and fresh. Then comes along some dufus that has to stink up someone's fresh, clean clothes. I think that is very inconsiderate of the smoker. And….DO NOT THROW YOUR CIG BUTTS OUT OF THE CAR WINDOW!! You're going to start a fire on the side of the road!! You should feel ashamed and guilty for throwing your lit cig butts out of your car window. If you don't have an ashtray, then use a coke can or something else. For crying out loud!!!

When you are in a public shopping place, please put things back properly after you've looked at it and decided not to buy it. I see these idiots unfolding pants, shirts, etc... and then just tossing them over the rack. Put it back the correct way, please!! Don't just leave a mess for someone else to fix. It doesn't matter that the stores have employees to right your wrong. It's stupid and bad manners to leave something a mess after you've touched it. Put it back the right way. Thank you. When you eat at a public fast food joint, please put your trash in the trash can and your tray in it's holder. I see people just get up and walk away and leave such a mess on the table, and on the floor.

Fast food places are not like big restaurants, where a waiter comes to take your order, and a bus boy comes to clean your mess. It is considered to be good mannered to clean up after yourself, and place your chairs back in close to the table. So people don't trip over them while walking to their table. Even though the fast food place has people to clean up after you. They have to, otherwise not only the health dept would come down on them, but it's bad for business to have a dirty, messy dining area.

Please, show your good manners and clean up after yourself and put your chair back close to the table. Thank you. 7) Baseball games. When the singing of our national anthem is going on. It is considered to be respectful and traditional to stand up, place your right hand on your heart, and take your hat off, during the singing of our national anthem. I think some respect for some of our traditions has been lost, and should be regained again. Thank you, and let's all bless America however you want to bless us, and enjoy the baseball game.

CHAPTER 4
MARRIAGE AND RELATIONSHIPS

Infidelity. Should we re-think our attitudes and traditions about marriage? We expect to remain faithful, but reality shows an alarming number cheat on their spouse. Should we just except this as natural behavior, even allow it? To relieve stress and daily fighting and arguing? We should expect it to happen, instead of hope it won't happen.

Are we fooling ourselves? In some cases, yes. I know it is possible for a couple that are meant to be together forever, are soul partners. Marriage is just a formality to them. But, for many others…it seems to feel like a trap. Perhaps we can think of a business relationship, instead of ownership complete with all the paperwork.

Why get married in the first place? Our religion rules it. Rules our lives? Why get married? So we can appear higher standard in society? We can look good. But underneath is a whole other world. And for some, it's a hell. If a young adult, age 18, of legal age, wants to get married, some, obviously not all, older people freak out and treat them as if getting married young is a huge mistake. But look at all the examples young people have to look to. Some older people seem to think that divorce is a big failure and mistake. That is because that is what their religion has told them.

But, to people that do not choose to follow a religion, but rather follow their hearts and the natural balance of human nature, divorce is not a failure, or mistake. It is a learning process in their lives. Nothing to feel bad about or freak out and panic about. See what some of these religions cause some people to do? Freak out and panic. That they have absolutely no control over the young couple, or no control over anyone at all. They who believe "their way", are happy when they can control other people.

We must never forget, that we live in a free country. Where the legal age is 18. Old enough to vote. Old enough to go off to war and either be killed, or come home alive. Too many people in our society come down very hard on young people if they want to live their own way. Again, it is the influence of some religion, that controls this attitude. Our way or you're wrong. That is exactly what these religions are trying to force on all of us.

There is a growing number of Americans that choose to shun religion, and live free. In free America. It is not against our laws for someone age 18 to get married. So, I say to these religious people….BACK OFF. TOO BAD. They cannot, and will not control the lives of free people. Your religion is YOUR option. Not law. And not to be forced on anyone.

Some, obviously not all, people think that you MUST follow this way to a "T", and cannot under any circumstances, bend or stray from living THIS particular religious way. Strict. Punishment.

Condemnation. Harassment. Abuse. Major Guilt Trips. Psychological Abuse. Once again, Free people will not subscribe to any way of life that feels more imprisoning, rather than allowing it's people to make their own choices. We are not buying into the ways of religion. We choose our way. More free. And just because we want to live free from religion or religious influence, DOES NOT in any way, make these free people any bad or worse than anyone else in the country. Free people are just as hard working and decent as anyone else.

We will never allow anyone to force their religion on us. And THAT is the tradition of the free people of the United States of America. Many of us see the hypocrisy that some, not all, but plenty, of religious people that hide behind their religion, and break their own rules. Child molestation is just one horrible reality. And all the divorces that these people continue to do. They say it's a failure, and extremely bad for their religious society, but they do it anyway. Again, I say, conform or be cast-out. Fit-in with everybody else. Free people do not believe in that, for the most part. They are unique. Not copy cat clones.

YOU WANT TO SEE SOMETHING FUNNY? Seems like most men think about sex a lot. Seems like they think of it most of the time. Take your man, your average, everyday man. While he's watching football or his favorite sport on tv. Wait until a long break in the program to talk to him. Now you should have his full attention. Let's say you just want to shoot the bull with him, tell him about your day. To keep him from being bored and drifting off while you are speaking, you may need to *sprinkle* your conversation. And every time you use that word, he twitches. It's just a natural response. He doesn't even realize he's doing it.

Your conversation might go something like this: You- "Hi honey, how was your *sex* day?" He twitches and looks up at you quizzically. Man- "It was fine, same as always". You-"My day was a little busy *sex*. I went down to the Mall *sex* to finish my Christmas shopping *sex*". He twitches every time you use that word *sex*. You just nonchalantly toss it in there, in no particular order or sense. Just sprinkling your speech with it. He looks a bit confused. And that is a cute look, don't you agree? You-"Yeah, I stuck a screwdriver *sex* in a jerk's tire, that cut in front of me *sex* and took the parking spot I was *sex* waiting for. The dumb jerk *sex*". And on and on you go until he decides he would be happy to give you some *sex*. But be careful how many times you use this on him. He'll be twitching so much it might cause him to have convulsions then you'll have to call 9-11!!

CHAPTER 5
COMMUNICATION BREAKDOWN

It's what you say, and how you say it. Banging my head again. This time with anger, confusion, and frustration. I must be doing something wrong. I cannot seem to communicate with people. They don't seem to understand what I'm saying or why? It's me that didn't understand at first. What I was dealing with. Over and over I kept running into the same stupid wall with people. I finally figured it out. I'm slow, but I eventually got it. I never stopped working the problem over in my head. Here is the typical scenario: Man or women asks young, female me a question. Simple enough you'd think. Harmless. Just a curious probe for information from this young women standing before them.

Seemingly an innocent question. Example: "So, what are you doing with yourself these days?". I reply. I give my simple, honest answer. "I'm working in a office during the day, and studying business at the junior college at night". Here's where the problem starts. They reply to my answer by saying a rude or criticizing comment. They insult me and then tell me I'm wrong for feeling insulted. One of the most common responses is telling me I'm wrong for doing what I'm doing. That I shouldn't be studying business, or working, or whatever I'm doing, they think it's wrong.

And I'm just trying to make a living and head in the direction I want to be going with my young life. I'm doing what's right for me. And they don't, and won't, see it that way. And then, after they insult me, they tell me I'm too sensitive. What??? I'm not that sensitive, I'm more flabbergasted and flustered. It generated the need for me to explain everything. And they would reply that I didn't need to explain. I was being defensive. A natural response to being insulted. All I did was just give a innocent answer. I didn't tell them what they wanted to hear. And they think that I got upset because THEY didn't tell me what I wanted to hear. You follow that?? It may take some effort. I just shake my head, say "whatever" and walk away. And I've been able to stay away from people like that.

No matter what I say to people that think (that) way, I will always be wrong in their eyes. They believe that they are "all wise". And I don't believe they are coming across in a very wise way! Part of the problem at the time was my youth. I've met too many older people that ASSUME young people do not know anything, have absolutely no experience, and that the older people have to give them guidance and tell them what to do with their lives.

Mold them and shape the young. Intelligent young people will be offended. What many, obviously not all, older people fail to realize is that young people generally don't care what you know. And young people are following their natural talents, and instincts for their own lives. They have a good idea of which direction they want to go. And the confusion comes when there are a lot of choices, and they may have trouble making up their minds. That's ok.

What are they, on some kind of time line or something? You must be this (occupation) before this age (pick a number), or else you are a huge failure. Wrong. People of all ages can try anything they want, and either like it, or drop it, and move on to the next thing in life. They will eventually find a place for themselves in this world.

But, we as a society, hardly allow young people the freedom to try out things before they settle on one choice or the other. And then our society treats them like they HAVE TO stay in that choice and are not allowed to change careers, jobs, schools, or whatever. I'm talking freedom here. Again, the religious influence even spills over onto young people at the time in their lives when they have choices to make, and choose to follow their hearts. I think too many older people have the effect of "beating young people over their heads" with the "you musts, and you must nots" or else pay the price, preaching at them all the time. No wonder why they rebel. I know they are being insulted.

Let them try things out, within reason. Drugs obviously are stupid. And they know it. But, as long as they stay away from doing stupid things like drugs, alcohol abuse, smoking cigarettes, or dope, and all those usual stupid things. I say let them follow their hearts and try things out. Let them chase their loves, talents, and dreams. Give young people the freedom, without hassling them all the time. If you stay away from drugs and stupid stuff, hell, you can be anything you want. If you're chasing the dream of music, acting, or whatever it is. You have the freedom to go for it.

Just keep away from the stupid stuff, and the stupid people, and you'll do just fine. Don't worry about failure. I think there is no such thing. I believe in stepping stones, not mistakes. No guilt trips. Live your dreams. Especially while they are young, energetic, physically strong and able, and mentally sharp. Young people are at their peak in life. Let them shine. Let them play. Let them be FREE!!!!!

So now I've learned. I'm not afraid to be just outright rude. I get the upper hand right away. Try to disarm them. With these type of "difficult and irritating" people, I reply to their supposed innocent question: "I'm not going to answer that, because you will say something stupid in response to my answer". Or "It's too complicated for you to understand". That's all they want. Is the opportunity to be superior. The opportunity to put someone down. I like to beat them to the punch. Or rather, I just like to stay away from people like that. I consider it a big waste of my time to have to deal with people like that on a regular basis. It's like I say, it's what you say, and how you say it. The tone of the comment is important. If you give it in a certain tone, it will be received that way. It's received how it's given.

And some people act all innocent like they didn't mean it that way. But, they SAID it in that tone and manner. So, what the hell do they expect? Of course the receiver will be insulted! I'm very thankful for the people than can communicate on an intelligent level. They can easily figure things out, and do not use a insulting tone or manner when speaking. They are secure in themselves and do not feel the need to put someone else down, to boost their ego or self-esteem. Some, not all, people judge people by how they look, how they are dressed. This is one of the biggest mistakes that are constantly made.

You think these people should know better than that by now? They get a idea of how a person is by how they are dressed. But they can be so very wrong about the individual. Again, I say, this is a free country. It's not against the law to dress how we please, within reason obviously. It's the religious influence again. The conform or be cast out attitude. How people dress, in my opinion, has nothing to do with their intelligence or competence.

Casual people are comfortable, smart and fun. I recommend, for those people that assume, to just be more careful. And, it would be nice if more of these negative people can be more relaxed and accepting. After all, they cannot control how people dress. It's not religious control here. It's freedom. How many people have felt misunderstood? What some people see on the outside, is just the clothing part of the person's personality. Inside, is a mind at work. Thinking, reading, questioning everything, logic, people study, music, love, hate, and more. I see too much in this country communication breakdown. Some people trying to control others.

CHAPTER 6
UNDERSTANDING TRUCK DRIVING
What Every Motorist Needs to Know

Includes: Cruisin' with Susan: Accidents (some graphic photos), Animals and Wonder
Moments * Heroes of the Highway * Trucker Buddy Program * Best & Worst Roads for
Driving, Designs, Signage, etc.. Best & Worst Drivers by City.

Many motorist don't realize how much they put themselves in danger, with regard to big rig
trucks. According to the NTSB (National Transportation Safety Board), 80% of all accidents
between cars and big rig trucks are caused by the drivers' of cars'. It is my feeling as well as
other truck drivers, that if the motoring public were better educated on big rig trucks, many
accidents can be prevented. Simply put, the car drivers' do not realize how they are
endangering themselves.

STOP BEHIND WHITE LINES For truck trailer turning clearance. As many of you have
experienced, if you over-shoot the white line, you don't leave enough room for a truck's
trailer to make the turn. So many motorists don't realize that it's THEY that are making the
mistake, not the truck driver. The motorists' honk their horns, flip the middle finger, and yell
at the truck driver. PLEASE, for your safety, you must STOP BEHIND THE WHITE
LINE. That is why the white line is positioned where it is.

For truck trailer turning clearance. The truck driver has to swing wide to make the turn, and
trailers always have a drag on them. If you see a trailer bearing down on you, and looking as
though it will run you over, look at your position in the street! Are you over the white line?
Well, no wonder it looks like you're going to get smashed. You have placed yourself in a
dangerous position. You are in the way.

It's not the truck driver's fault that you over-shot the white line. People are always quick to
blame the truck driver. When they don't even realize what they (the driver of the car) have
done wrong. Spend a week in the driver seat of a big rig, and you'll change your car driving
habits. Only then will you understand what so many 4-wheelers are doing wrong out there.
And they (car drivers) don't even realize it. Truck drivers' are in your city or town for a
reason. They are earning a living picking up and delivering every kind of freight. If you got it,
a trucker brought it. The car you drive, the food you eat, the bed you sleep in, your clothes,
your home entertainment, gasoline, and everything.

All the things in your life that you use, need and want. They haul the freight, that stocks the
shelves of the stores you enjoy shopping at. In shopping malls, please understand that semis'
are not there to go shopping. They are delivering washers, dryers, refrigerators, clothes,
riding mowers, etc.. So when you see a semi, don't give them the finger, rather, give them
the right of way. They are working for you. There are customers' waiting for these items. It's
no picnic for a semi to have to maneuver a 53' trailer with approx 20' sleeper cab, 13'6"
high, and 8' wide. It's S.T.U.N.T. driving for big rigs.

A professional driver can move around without hitting anyone or anything. If motorists only knew what today's professional truck drivers' have to go through to get their cdl's, (commercial driver license). They would have a new respect for them. First, they go through one month, 5 days a week, 40hr a week truck driving school. Tuition averages $3000.00 and up for the whole term. Some drivers' have been able to qualify for a government program called J.T.P.A. (Job Training Partnership Act), of which I qualified for.

Under this program, the government pays the tuition and the student not only has to complete the school, but stay employed for a pre-determined amount of time. In the field of their schooling. This is a good example of our country giving opportunity to those less fortunate. So that they may improve their income and employment opportunities. Thus turning a low paying job, living paycheck to paycheck, into a future homeowner. Better pay = better opportunities. And by the time the student qualifies and takes the program, he/she has already paid well over $3000.00 in income taxes as well as purchase taxes.

So, in essence, the student tax payer has actually paid their own tuition. It doesn't technically come from other Americans taxes. If you think about it. They are getting something good from the government, besides living in a free country. At end of school, students take the cdl test at their local dmv. On average 7-8 written tests, including air brakes, double and triple trailers, hazmat, tankers, and regular driving tests. A drug and medical exam.

Then after they pass all the written tests, they take a air brake test. They have to pass that. Then a full truck and trailer inspection inside and out test. Pass that. They do a difficult and very involved challenging backing test around cones, from all angles. Most people fail this test, several times. If you fail just one of these tests, you don't go any further. You have to start all the tests, all over again.

The last test usually is the long, drive around town, driving test. Watch your trailer while turning. Watch your speed. Use your turn signals. Watch out for traffic, merging, lane changes, etc… With the examiner stone faced right next to you for all your tests. And there is no sweet talking these examiners. They are borderline mean. When a trailer is making a turn, the rear portion of it side tracks. That is why drivers' have to take up two lanes to make a turn. And swing wide. When you are out in traffic and behind a big rig, watch the rear of the trailer as the driver makes the turn. You'll see exactly what I'm talking about. The driver is not blocking two lanes just to piss you off.

They need that space to clear the corner, stop sign, traffic light, person standing waiting to cross street, etc.. If they turn too sharp, the back of the trailer side tracks and wipes out whatever is in it's way. So please, again, give the driver assistance, and give clearance. Stay back to allow the driver room to make the turn. Please be patient. The more car drivers in the way, the longer it's going to take the truck driver to clear them all and make the turn.

This is another area that 4-wheelers don't realize why the truck driver is doing what they are doing. Why they swing wide, etc.. Stay back and give him some room. They appreciate your help. You can even take a child's toy big rig and see what I mean. Set up a street situation and maneuver the toy around.

MERGING means either speed up or slow down depending on your speed and the speed of the vehicles already on the highway. It doesn't mean ride along the right side of a Semi and try to make the semi move over so you can get over. Or it doesn't mean speed up like a race car driver and cut in front of the Semi because you don't want to be behind it.

Just before your lane runs out. You'll clip the front bumper of the truck and go flying off the road, into the ditch or worse. For one thing, big rig trucks cannot slow down fast. We have a lot of weight and speed we are moving. It takes the length of a football field for a Semi to come to a complete stop at the average speed of 65 mph. The heavier the load is, the longer it takes to stop. Motorists that merge improperly, do not realize what is on the left of the truck driver.

Car drivers' cannot see what's in the left lane next to the truck. If the Semi doesn't move over, it's because someone is in that lane. And the semi isn't going to push them out of the way so that you can get over. That is where you, the merger, either needs to speed up or slow down and let the truck pass, to merge onto the highway safely. We get so many each day that run right along the right side of us, trying to outrun us to the end of the onramp, and cut over in front of us. The car drivers slam on their brakes when they realize they can't make it. And then they have the audacity to blame the truck driver. We are not driving your car.....YOU ARE. The 4-wheelers are putting themselves as well as the truck driver who also has a family, in danger of a collision.

Unfortunately, too many motorists have the feeling and attitude that trucks are at fault, and that trucks think they own the road. If motorists only knew, they would change their driving habits. They would realize, "Oh, it's not the truck driver in most cases, it's me". Now, I'm not saying all truck drivers' don't do wrong. Some do. But when they are caught, they pay a heavy fine, or lose their license. Truck drivers' are federally regulated. And can be pulled over and inspected any time a dot (dept of transportation) officer wants to pull them over.

Check the log book, insurance, registration, fuel tax card, cdl, medical certificate, brakes, lights, horns, cleanliness, fire extinguisher, inside and out of the truck, cab, and trailer. Full inspection. Including a on the spot drug test. Cops don't need a reason to pull trucks over. Like tail light out, registration, seat belt, or any other reason. Trucks and the drivers are federally regulated. So that is why there are more professional truck drivers on the roads today than years before. Big companies provide training, quality equipment, drug tests, background tests, good pay, stock options, medical, 401k, and so many other benefits. There are fewer ratty looking independent owners out there.

The standards for trucking have escalated to the highest possible standards in the country for the past 20-30 years or so. And the standards are always climbing, as high as possible. Tighter control. Stricter discipline, fines, imprisonment, etc.. When we say "professional truck driver" we mean it. Well trained and as safe as possible.

Today's truck drivers have a professional attitude, for the most part, and the pride that comes with driving a big rig. We tolerate the constant, daily mistakes that 4-wheelers make. Most truck drivers have learned patience. Just let the 4-wheeler go, without punishment. For they know not what they do. We just shake our heads and move on, as safely as possible.

Truckers' are the heroes of the highway. If you are ever in a accident, or need help, most of the time a trucker is the first one to pull over and help you out. We take pride in that. As you can see, not all truck drivers are ugly, nasty, unkempt, dirty, stinky, greasy, homeless looking, bums and creeps. Most are clean, as showers are available at home, truck terminals, and all truck stops. They are men, women, of varying ethnic groups, and ages. And all are hard workers. Putting in long days. As noted before, truckers' are federally regulated.

We can't drive no more than 11hrs straight in a day, and must take 10hrs straight off for rest. We can't work more than 14hrs a day, combined driving and loading, unloading service. And no more than 70hrs in a 7day period. We typically cover between 500-700 miles a day. And minimum 3,000 miles a week. Which earns us from $700-1000.00 a week, depending on company and years of experience. As of this date. And most companies provide a food per diem. We get reimbursed for a certain cost of food each day. We generally stay out on the road approx 3-4weeks at a time, then take 3-5 days off. Depending on the company. If we're not moving, we're not making any money. We get paid by the mile.

And live in our sleeper cabs, shower at truck stops, and rest every chance we can. So, you want to be a truck driver? No dui's, no felonies, and eat a big breakfast, because it's going to be a long day. No matter how hard a truck driver may push his endurance level, he/she won't make that much more money. And it's not worth killing yourself over. No freight is worth dying for. We're not going to get rich doing this job. We have no reason to push too hard.

Just kick back, take your loads, get all the rest, and enjoy life. Many truckers use this opportunity to buy land, home, boats, cars, etc… so they can enjoy them later on. It makes no sense to pay rent on a place you'd only use once a month. Best to buy land or home, that way you own it. Many drivers' follow this route. Of course, people with families are a different story. Their own personal situation. Whatever works well for them.

<u>DON'T SPEED UP!! LET ME OVER!!</u> This happens to all of us. We have our turn signal on, trying to change lanes because we need to, and someone in the lane you are trying to get into, speeds up to cut you off. Then they honk and cuss at *you* as though you cut them off!! Now you're pissed, they are pissed and it could get worse. Or, you're trying to get over, and the person BEHIND you changes lanes into the lane you're trying to get into, then speeds up to cut *you* off! And then has the nerve to act angry as if you were the one that cut them off.

And you're both pissed at each other. People, listen. We know what you're doing and why. Don't put yourself in danger by trying to purposely cut someone off that had the right of way to begin with. DON'T SPEED UP ON PURPOSE TO BLOCK THEM!! You put them and you in a accident situation. Not to mention some road rage. There is no reason to be in such a hurry. If you're late, you're late. Too bad. You can't do anything about it. Get up earlier in the morning. Don't take it out on other motorists on the road. Patience, goes a long way.

Less stress, less wear and tear on your car. Truckers plan their trips accordingly. So we don't need to rush, or be in a panic, or stress. Many truck drivers' don't like going into big cities if we can help it. Too many of the motorists are buzzing around like psycho bees, rushing, cutting everyone off, not letting people over, and are in too much of a hurry. We have to wade through the traffic mess. We'd rather go around whenever we have the opportunity.

You'd think that if you live in a big city, where there is a lot of traffic, you'd know better by now that patience is better than stressing yourself out and being in such a panic rush all the time. What good is it hurrying around like that every day? Beating yourself and your car up? I grew up in Los Angeles. I know all too well the stupidity and nonsense of rushing around in traffic. You practically use your car as a weapon. Rushing to not let someone change lanes in front of you, etc.. That's stupid. Relax, let em' over. What's the damn hurry?? Now that I've driven a Semi for over 5 years, I drive my car somewhat the same way.

I'm slower than I was before truck driving. Not too slow. But I do the speed limit most times. I don't feel the need anymore to be in the panic rush of traffic. I just kick back and cruise it. I let people over. I slow to posted 35, or 45 mph so vehicles can get in and out of travel lanes, driveways, shopping centers, etc.. Slow down, and traffic will actually move better.

Do this experiment. 1. Do the posted speed limit and watch how it effects the traffic around you. 2. Keep a relatively long distance space between you and the vehicle in front of you, when you are stuck in traffic. Yes, somebody will most likely cut in, because they think that it's a opening. But if you stay back a bit, you may be able to keep rolling. But if you hug the bumper of the car in front of you, then you'll do the accordion affect. Forward, stop. Forward, stop. And so on. Stay back, and keep rolling. And for those that cut in to these so-called openings, stop doing that. You're not going to get ahead in the traffic. You're only helping to cause it to slow down.

That's why it's slow because people have to hit the brakes for people cutting in front of them. And cutting in at the last minute too. Merge earlier, stay in your lane unless you're exiting, and don't cut in front of people. Try to combat the accordion effect. 3. In traffic in cities and towns, slow down to the posted speed limit. Say, if it's 35, for example. And watch how much easier it is for cars and trucks to pull out into traffic lanes.

DON'T PASS ON RIGHT! During a truck's wide right turn to clear a street corner, or trying to get into a driveway. And especially in traffic. Some drivers' will scare you on purpose if you try to sneak by on the right while they are turning. To teach you a lesson. Be patient, or be hurt. During traffic on any road, but especially freeways, interstates. A truck may go around stopped vehicles on the side of the road.

Like police cars, broken down vehicles, tow trucks, etc.. for safety. So the trucks don't side swipe the people there. Then, in a short time, the truck will get back in the far right lane, unless it's a exit only, another freeway, or something. HERE'S WHERE MOTORISTS GET THEMSELVES INTO TROUBLE. They get impatient and want to zoom around the right side of the truck.

Right at the same time the truck driver decides to get back over into the far right land. Now the motorist is in his/her truck's blind spot. And can be run off the road into a ditch, trees, off a bridge, or anywhere. Don't put yourself in harm's way. Flash your lights to get the truck back over. But don't get in the right land. Stay where you are. Sometimes, actually, a lot of the time, trucks tend to almost wait too long to get back over.

Leaving an opening for a 4-wheeler to jump in the right land. When he/she finally decides to get over, your are sitting there, and he/she may not see you. Although they have 2-3 mirrors on that side, you still could be sitting in the blind spot. STAY OUT OF THERE!! And as a general rule, IF YOU CAN'T SEE THE TRUCK'S MIRRORS, THE DRIVER CAN'T SEE YOU. Stay out of harm's way and blind spots. Don't put yourself in danger.

DON'T PARK IN TRUCK PARKING!!! at rest areas and travel centers. Cars and van can go anywhere, where as trucks cannot. Smaller vehicles are taking a spot from a tired truck driver, and one that also must stop driving by law. According to the driver's log book. If you are driving a vehicle and towing a trailer of any kind, or driving a truck and towing a car. It's ok for the additional vehicle in your party to park behind you, and your trailer, IN THE SAME PARKING SPOT. Instead of taking up two parking spaces with all your vehicles.

TRUCKERS 4 AMERICA   We truck drivers are keeping our eyes and ears open for any suspicious people or activity. Our government has given truckers' a special 800# to call and report. We cover every mile of this country every day. And we see a lot. Motorists drinking alcohol (beer) and driving. Smoking pot while driving, etc.. We are watching you!! We still have problems with people driving while holding a cell phone with one hand. You are a danger to yourself and everybody around you when you do that.

Invest $10-20 and get yourself a hands free device. They make them in all styles, for comfort and reliability. They can go in your ear, on your ear, or like stereo headphones, over your head and softly on your ear. You will be a lot safer on the road if you invest in a much needed hands free cell phone device. If you can afford the phone and the bill, you can afford to get a hands free. One other thing of noteworthy importance. Many trucks, especially those of major companies, are speed governed. Computer controlled speed limit.

Some are governed to go no faster than 60 or 65, and some 70. So if you notice a truck trying to pass, and can't seem to. Then you know it's a speed governed truck.

CRUISIN' WITH SUSAN
Includes: Accidents, Animals and Wonder Moments

Five years and counting. I've been driving a Semi around the lower 48 states and Toronto, Canada. Never a dull moment. I've seen some interesting and horrific things. And beautiful country, as well as best and worst city road designs. Sometimes people ask me if I've ever been in an accident. I tell them about San Francisco, Ca one summer day.

I was just fresh from training. Barely on my own for one week. Happily going to work with my boxer (at the time) dog Brandy with me. I get a load delivering in San Francisco.

I wanted so much to show my bosses that I can deliver in that small and hilly city. No problem. I knew it would be a challenge, and I was eager to prove myself. I've been to San Francisco several times by car. And it can be tough for a car, let alone a Semi. My cab was approx 20' long with sleeper, and my trailer was a 53' long dry van, 14' high. Full of pallets of toilet paper and paper towel packages for a chain grocery store. I had to make four stops in one day, and the last four stops the next day. All in the same city. I didn't make it through the first day. I handled the hills ok, I had good training and practice.

What stopped me was the landing gear on my trailer got stuck on a flower bed curb in the store parking lot, as I was trying to exit after delivery. I wound up burning up the main rear end differential and had to use the second rear end to get the truck to the shop in nearby Oakland. After all my attempts to free myself from this situation, my company sent a tow truck to lift the trailer just 2 inches so I could get free! All this because a guy had his car parked on the street, sticking out about a foot into the driveway.

And I was trying to swing as wide as I could so I don't clip his car. After I was free, he came up to me as asked "Do you need me to move my car?". "YES!!" I said, a bit flustered. I tried to smile and be professional. But I felt like smacking the guy for his parking mistake. He moved, and I was able to get out into the street, and limp my way to Oakland. But this little incident wasn't even the worst of it. Oh no. That was yet to come. I got to the shop in Oakland and the guy told me to drop my 14' high, 53' long trailer down the street, along a curb.

Then bring my truck in for repairs. By this time it was 10pm and I was very tired. I'd been up since 5am and running pretty hard. It was the end of June, with the 4th of July just around the corner. I drove around the block and found what I thought was a good spot to drop my trailer. Plenty of room so I won't hit a parked car or anything. I was looking forward to a night of rest. It was dark, I was tired. But I stuck to my training (G.O.A.L.) Get Out And Look. Before backing, and I did. I saw a parked car that was far enough away. I also saw a power pole on the sidewalk. No concern of mine, I won't be jumping the curb.

I'll be on the street. I have plenty of practice and training. So after checking that all was clear, I got back in my truck and started backing. I hardly moved when suddenly I heard TWO LOUD EXPLOSIONS!! "BOOM! BOOM!" And saw sparks flying every where. Power lines went down and were sparking "cheeech cheeech" all over the ground. It scared the piss out of me (literally, I had no bladder control), and I panicked and drove the truck with trailer still attached as fast as I could away from there.

Before I pulled away though, I saw a cop coming in the opposite direction from where I was facing. He drove over the live, sparking, fallen power lines and it scared the crap out of him too. And he sped off as fast as he could. He went one way, I went the other. He came fast to the scene as he must have been really close and heard the explosions.

I looked up the street at a big hotel and all the lights went off, as well as all the street lights. Then the hotel's reserve power kicked in. When I finally parked my truck, several blocks away, I was shaking so bad, it took me about half an hour to stop shaking. I cleaned myself up and changed my pants. Then took my dog for a careful walk, back to the scene. As I approached the scene, a fireman stopped me and said "Stand back ma'm, there's live power lines here". I stood nearby and watched.

And I saw something that gave my heart another jolt. A pile of wood. And I immediately thought it was my trailer that burned to the ground after I had dropped it. I thought the sparking power lines landed on the roof and it caught fire and burned the entire trailer to the ground. Then I realized what it was and calmed myself down. I was in a panic. It was the power pole that blew up when the top corner of my trailer hit the transformer box and exploded. Causing the pole to blow into pieces too. It couldn't of been my trailer, it was a few blocks away. I was a shaking, scared mess. As I stood there staring at it, a cop walked by right in front of me. I heard him say into his radio "We're looking for a (company name) driver".

He mentioned the name of the company I worked for then, and currently still work for. I knew I was just going to be fired as soon as my boss found out. Well, I thought, so much for truck driving. Better hit the want ads as soon as I get home. I called the officer to me and admitted that "I'm the driver you're looking for". He stood over me, about 10' tall, and I was about two inches tall and just glared at me.

I think he was surprised to see a small women that drives a huge truck. He quickly composed himself and glowered at me. Asking me all the pertinent questions. Like "what the hell happened here lady?". I took him over to my trailer and showed him that I did not, in fact, hit the pole, but I hit the transformer box, of the pole that was leaning in towards the street by a couple feet (probably due to earthquakes), and the box was low on the pole just enough for me to hit it. If I had a 13'6" high trailer, I bet you I wouldn't of hit that damn thing.

There were no wood chips embedded in the corner of my trailer. He thought I jumped the curb. I most certainly did not. And the city had part blame for the mislocation I like to call it, of the pole and box. I was not cited in this incident, and the cop eventually let me mope off to the shop. Boy, what a hell of a night.

The next day I saw the power company workers replacing the pole. It was about a 20' high pole with the new transformer box about at the top. And the new pole was leaning more straight, definitely away from the street. Way out of the way. As it turned out, my dog and I wound up getting a ride back to L.A. from another of our company's driver's.

I walked into the boss's office with my tail between my legs. I knew I was going to be fired. But I was in for a surprise. I actually had a cool boss. Both of them. They went to bat for me with headquarters. And I was able to keep my job. After one week off while my truck was being repaired, I got a ride back to Oakland to pick it up.

During that week off, it was 4th of July, and I would jump out of my skin every single time I heard a firecracker go off. Or the fireworks booming in the sky at night. Needless to say, I did not have a fun 4th that year!! The good part was I spent the holiday at my friend's place in Cerritos and we had bbq and relaxed in the Jacuzzi and had a good time. Brandy and I survived ok. But I'll never forget it. And I have not had a bad accident like the scale of that one, since. About one year later, in Dallas, Tx my 10yr old boxer dog Brandy died of cancer and kidney failure. She was a great dog and wonderful companion. I will make a memorial to her on my property.

15 MINUTES

On one sunny day a few years ago in Kansan, I was flagged down by a motorist needing a fire extinguisher for a crashed 4x4 pickup truck. I pulled over and ran to the scene. The fire was out so I didn't need to use my fire extinguisher. At first, I didn't notice where the driver was. He was passing this rv at a high rate of speed, lost control, and flipped his pickup truck several times.

I looked in the cab that landed in the upright position and saw the seat belt unused. I reached in and turned off his ignition. Looking at the rv driver and his wife, I asked "Where is he?". They had a grim look on their faces and pointed to the ground. The driver of the pickup truck was thrown from his vehicle and pinned underneath it. I looked around and saw his legs sticking out from under the pickup. He lay on his stomach. The muffler was burning a hole in his lower back and his legs were paper white and twisted over and over like a licorice stick. Judging by all the tools strewn about, he was in the plumbing business. A young, white man. He jeans stayed belted on as well as his boxer shorts stayed in place.

The rest of his pants looked as though someone took a razor blade and sliced lengthwise from his waist to his ankles. Several times on each leg. Exposing his underwear, bare legs, socks, and boots. His jeans were shredded. His boots stayed on his feet, and both his feet lay resting pointed in the same direction. I thought he was dead. The rv couple were quiet. He was still barely alive. I climbed down on my stomach near his head to talk to him.

I couldn't get down too close, there wasn't enough room between the ground and the under carriage of his truck. I spoke gently to him. Trying to comfort him. Telling him to hang on, help is on the way. Try to relax, everything's going to be ok. He couldn't breathe with the weight of the truck on his back, and his twisted and torn body pinned. He could only bob his head and grunt. I heard his clear, deep male voice. The front axle of his truck lay about 100 yards away. And the rear axle differential unit was torn away.

Both axles had differentials, that's how we could tell it was a 4x4 truck. Help arrived. It seemed to take a long time for them to get there, but I'm sure it was only 10-15 minutes. By the time the rescuers pulled him out, he had stopped moving. He was dead. His arms had been pulled from his shoulders. He lay face down with his head turned away.

They covered him up, and put him on a gurney. Loaded him into a waiting ambulance. No need to hurry. This unfortunate accident that I came upon is the worst I've seen yet. His seat belt lay in his cab, not used. Had he been wearing it, would he still be alive today? I like to think so. He lay there, hurt badly. It took him about 15 minutes to die.

A COLORADO MOMENT

On a winter morning a few years ago, I had a Colorado moment. One of those awe inspiring, spiritual experiences. I was headed west on US Hwy 160 from the I-25, and stopped to spend the night in a gravel lot in a small town called Del Norte. It was very dark when I pulled in. I took my dog Rowan for a walk, then went to bed. I didn't realize the beauty around me until sunrise the next morning.

I got up, rubbed the sleep from my eyes, and looked around. With a morning can of diet pepsi (my coffee), I took my dog for a quick walk. There was a large stream not 100' from where I parked. Lined with tall pine trees. That alone was beautiful scenery. Fresh air, the sound of the running water, peace and tranquility. We got back into the truck, and just as I was pulling out onto the highway, I wasn't even completely in the road yet, I experienced something magical. It's the only way I can find to describe it. A very large herd of antlered elk crossed my path. I started counting them right away, and lost count at 20 or so. They were big and beautiful. They crossed right in front of my truck Their antler's were taller than my hood. I held Rowan back so she couldn't see them. Otherwise she would of barked like a psycho at them. And I didn't want to ruin the moment. They crossed from my right to my left, walking along the stream I had just walked my dog near. It seemed to take a long time for them all to cross.

And finally, the last elk crossed the road in front of my truck, and joined his fellows down by the water. I was in awe, and watched them until I could see them no more. What a fantastic way to start the day! This was a real nature treat. My own personal Colorado Moment.

IGUANA CROSSING

July 2004. I was driving my car with my dog Rowan accompanying me, down to Key Biscayne, Florida from my home near Gainesville, Florida. I had four days home time off from work, so I decided to take a mini vacation. The first night we spent at a Motel 6 in Ft. Lauderdale. I use Motel 6 exclusively because they always allow dogs. The next morning Rowan and I ate breakfast and headed south to Miami. To the Rickenbacker Causeway and Key Biscayne. The color of the water is a clear turquoise color. And just looking at it invites you in. I wanted to explore this part of the state that I had not been to before.

The drive on the causeway is beautiful. Trees of all kinds line the road where there is land, and mangrove trees drink in the water and sun. You can literally pull your car over to a limestone parking spot right next to the water and go for a swim. Stay all day if you like. Bring a picnic lunch, or eat from one of the nearby snack bars. You won't go hungry here.

I snapped a lot of photos and continued on. My goal was to go to the end of the line. The very end of this island is Bill Blass State Park. As I was driving down the palm tree lined road, I had to stop suddenly so as to not hit the car stopped in front of me. In both lanes all traffic was stopped for some reason that I did not immediately see the reason.

Then I saw it, making a mad dash across the front bumper of the car in front of me. It was a huge green Iguana. As big as a cat easily. I was amazed at this site. Just out in the open, running around wild. Natural Florida blending in with development. They say that there are a lot of Iguanas that just run wild around there. It's just a normal thing for the residents and visitors to that area. I got a kick out of it. "Wow", I thought, "That's cool".

I couldn't get my camera out fast enough to snap a picture of it. And Rowan was barking at it like she was going to eat it, and the Iguana scurried faster and into the nearby bushes. I continued on into the park. It was early Saturday morning and I had all day to explore. I love to explore new places and am always curious as to what's over there, or what's on the other side. I like to get as full a experience as I can. Sometimes to the detriment of my fellow travelers. So I just leave them and go on my own. I won't let anyone get in my way of checking things out. It's not like we're handcuffed to each other!! We can always just meet back up later at a designated spot.

I drove all through the park and settled on my first spot for looking around. I had followed a sign that said "Boat Docks & Café". Yeah, sounds good to me. This little place was tucked in a cove off the main road. Rowan and I were hungry for some breakfast. And what a nice place this was. Amid palms, pines and mangroves sat a cute two story bar and café just feet from the wrap around, u-shaped dock. You'd pull your boat up, tie up, and walk up the dock to the bar and café, fill up and get back to boating.

There were a few really nice boats docked when we got there. I got a plate of bacon for Rowan and some eggs over hard, bacon, rye toast and orange juice for me. I also always bring a liter of spring water with me. And I carried Rowan's water bowel for her. Setting it down at short intervals so she can have plenty to drink. It was about 9am at the time and already 90 degrees with 90% humidity. Hot and muggy, exotic tropical weather. The water was the color I love the most. Crystal clear blue azure. Just like you see in the travel brochures.

After breakfast we walked around to the far point that connects with the Atlantic ocean. The islands of the Bahamas not too far away. Since it was just so hot, and I always wear something to swim in, Rowan and I decided to jump into the blue, warm, tropical water for a swim. My dog is a chow-shepherd mix and she loves to swim. She knows the word "swimming". I say to her "Let's go swimming", and she gets all excited and jumps around. The water was the perfect temperature, 80 degrees and salty.

Next time I must bring a floating lounge chair. Sunscreen and bug spray are also essential every day items to have with you at all times in Florida. As Rowan and I walked back to the car, we passed a forest of trees and brush. All very picturesque, jungle like. It was safe enough for me to let Rowan off the leash and run around and explore a bit. There were no other people or dogs around this area. With the exception of some rustling in the bushes. I like to imagine that the rustling was that of more iguanas.

I didn't see any more that day. Or any other kind of animal. We did more exploring and photo taking. Including the beautiful historic lighthouse that sits on the tip of the island. To get to the lighthouse, you park in the shady parking lot and walk past all the picnic tables, in the shade, and out to the swimming beach, and you see the lighthouse. As a wet dog and I got back in the car, we headed back to the causeway. And stopped along the way to park and do more swimming by the roadside.

I walked over to a nearby food snack bar and bought a huge Cuban meat sandwich. Which my dog was all too eager to help me eat. She can be a real "piglet" sometimes. After lounging around in the water for a little while longer, with the Miami skyline in our background. I decided since I was this close, why not head over to Key Largo. Go poking around in the stores and beach areas for awhile. I still had a lot of daytime left. It was a Saturday, and everybody and their boat had the same idea. I was one of many cars stuck in the small two lane traffic jam for more than an hour.

I was beginning to think it was a bad idea to head down to Key Largo on a Saturday. I eventually made it into the town and stopped at the first big pink tourist place I came upon. Shell World. I enjoy buying cute tacky tourist gifts and souvenirs at places like these. After a half hour, while Rowan sat in air conditioned car all wet from her swimming, I walked out loaded down with several bags of goodies. I got a pirate flag, a pretty pink conch shell, a cd of steel drum music, a cute brightly colored painted metal Caribbean home wall hanging with the words "Home Sweet Home" on it. And several more tropical and nautical decorations for my home.

With my newly acquired treasures stowed in my trunk, I took off for a little more exploring. I came upon a jet ski rental place on the gulf side of the island. It had a restaurant and a beach bar area. I grabbed my camera and moved in for a closer look. With Rowan on the leash, I walked around the place, and we also took a dip in the water, splashing around the dock and mangroves. So here I am, just nosing around, not going to rent a jet ski, this time, but just scoping out the place. I get some looks from people, but nobody bothered us. As if tourists always just wandered in off the street and went swimming around their docks.

When we emerged from the water looking like drowned rats, a young man, jet ski employee approached us. He was very nice and friendly and played with my dog a bit. Then he pointed to a hose at the dock so we can rinse the salt water off us. I thanked him. This looked like a good place to come back to in the future. After a full day of swimming, eating, exploring and shopping, I gassed up my car in Key Largo and headed north to Ocala. Where my Semi truck is parked at work. It took me about 6 hours to drive from Key Largo to Ocala. We arrived about 11:00 pm. Rowan & I were exhausted. We lay our weary heads down in the sleeper cab bed, and fell fast asleep. Rowan taking up most of the small twin bed. It's back to work in the morning. Dreaming of more sun and surf.

THE HOT SEAT

Sept 2004. I was driving my Semi truck and loaded trailer, northbound on I-95 in Virginia when a scary thing happened. A little green car pulled in front of me and exploded. We were just cruising along for awhile, everything normal. Then all of a sudden I am nearly blinded by thick white smoke and all I can see of the little green car is a ball of fire coming from underneath the car. The driver of the car quickly pulled off the road and jumped out. I was carrying a very heavy load and could not stop quick enough to pull over and help him.

I had done all I could to avoid running him right over. For a moment I was certain that I was going to smash right into him. It takes the length of a football field to stop a big rig. I saw in my rearview mirrors that another car quickly pulled over to aide him. It took me several minutes to calm my breathing and heart rate. I don't know what caused the explosion, but I'm glad the guy is alright. His car was completely covered in flames in a matter of minutes. Whew! Just another day at the office!

AMISH IN AMERICA

One night as I was driving down a back county road in Pennsylvania, I noticed something moving in the dark shadows. I couldn't make out exactly what it was. I knew it was big. I put on my 4way flashers and slowed down. When in doubt, be safe. "What is it?" I asked myself. I crawled slowly toward the dark, moving object. Looks like a big head moving up and down. Still not sure what it was, I nearly came to a full stop in the road.

It was pitch black dark in this rural part of the state. Then the moving thing came out into the road, slowly. It was then that I noticed what it was, Amish horse and buggy. When he turned in front of me, my headlights shown on the reflectors on the rear of the buggy. Oh, I thought. That's what it is. A horse, black, bobbing his head up and down, waiting to pull out into the road. I wasn't going to move and take a chance on hitting it, them.

Until I was sure. They drove along the road for a mile or two then pulled off into a feed store parking lot. I'm told the Amish are not supposed to drive their horse and buggy at night, for this particular reason. Most people can't see them until it's too late. Not long ago I was in Indiana on a cold, snowy, winter day. I pulled into a Wal-Mart parking lot to do my usual shopping. I like that I can usually park my rig there and be out of the way.

As I was moving to my spot, I noticed what looked like a barn of sorts off into the far corner of the parking lot. I took a closer look and realized that it was special parking for the Amish and their horses and buggies. "Wow, cool", I thought. I took some photos of this parking barn, and while I was snapping away, a family pulled up in their Amish ride. Horse and buggy. The family dressed like pilgrims. "Cool". I took photos of them as well. How about that. In modern times, Wal-Mart, Semi trucks, and Amish horse and buggy parking. Quite the contrast, I thought.

SLIP N' SLIDE MICHIGAN

Pouring rain, wind blowing sideways at 30 mph, bouncy road, and empty trailer. Going down the road at 60mph. Recipe for a crash. And I almost had one. Scared the crap out of me. I had to go empty (we call that deadhead) for 350 miles that day to get to the shipper by midnight. Not the best weather, but there isn't anything drivers can do about it. Cruising along, trying to make good time, when suddenly I felt something wrong.

I looked in my rearview mirror and saw my trailer swinging around to my left. "Oh shit" I said. I then proceeded to do about 10 things at once and attempt to straighten out my trailer and avoid a crash. I let off the accelerator, didn't hit my brakes, I must of downshifted, I'm not sure. I steered into the turn, cussed some more. And did other things that I can't exactly remember. For a split second there, I was looking right at the grass medium. The middle of the highway had a incline of about 10 degrees then flattened out in the middle. You go down a slight embankment. If you are unlucky that is. A car might be ok going down that, but not a semi. We are top heavy and tip over easily. I braced for impact.

I was trying to line my truck up so I can hit the medium and try to at least come to a stop standing straight up. Not tipped over. No rollovers for me, thank you. Somehow, I managed to straighten my trailer out just in time. I didn't even have time to panic. I don't know what my dog Rowan was doing during all this. I hope she sensed what was going on and was trying to brace herself for impact as well. I got back in line and immediately felt my heart racing. I thought it would bust through my chest. I looked in my mirrors and realized that I impacted two other vehicles on the road. I didn't hit anyone, but I made a red pickup truck go into the medium, and he kept driving and got back on the road after I straightened out. I waved a "I'm so sorry" gesture at him, and he waved back "It's ok".

And then got the hell away from me as fast as he could. The other vehicle I jeopardized was another semi. Right behind me. He managed to slow down so we don't tangle. He was a good driver. I got on the cb and told him I'm really sorry about that. And he said "No prob. Good save driver". I told him I was empty and bouncing, losing traction, on this bad road. He said he understood, then passed me and put some distance between us. Needless to say that spooked the hell out of me. Still pouring rain, bouncy bad road, wind blowing sideways at 30mph, I continued on my way to the shipper at.....45mph. For about 100 miles!! I was scared half to death. I managed to make it to the shipper.....at 11:45pm! 15 minutes to spare!!

The customer understood and loaded my trailer fast. They let me sleep there overnight and head out early in the morning. From then on, I slow down in rain. Even more. I average about 55mph in the rain. I'm still a bit spooked, even a couple years later. They aren't kidding when they say "Slippery When Wet". It's not a experience I ever want to have happen again.

Next time, I may not be so lucky.

TALKING ABOUT SLIPPERY...

Welcome to Miami. Hot. And rainy in the afternoons. On one such afternoon, I was heading southbound on the I-95 when I noticed a "patch" of rain up ahead. I'd say it was about a mile of rain. Dry, then rain for about a mile, then dry again. Kinda weird but that's Florida for ya. Being as I had plenty of time to prepare for it, I slowed down. Especially after that Michigan incident still fresh in my bones. I slowed to about 55mph and was in the middle of three lanes.

I seemed to be the only vehicle that slowed for this little bit of rain. No matter how much or how little, rain is rain, and when wet, roads will become slippery. And people seem to find this out the hard way! Suddenly a little blue car on my right, passing me started to spin out. Around and around it went, where it stops anyone knows. Round and round she goes. Well, she went around, right in front of me and I didn't smash her to smithereens because I had slowed down. She continued to spin out to my left and wound up landing upright in the medium ditch. But, on my left, in the left lane was a brand new caddy. I thought I would have cars bouncing off me on my right, on my left and all over.

I thought for sure this Cadillac would slam on his brakes to avoid hitting the little blue car, then spin out and wind up going under my trailer and so on. A big chain-reaction crash that would wind up on the evening news. As it turned out, the little blue car was the only one near me that crashed. We all continued on our way. Accelerating as we got onto the dry road. You never know when you are going to slide. But it's best not to in the first place. I'm sure you would agree. And so would the people in the little blue car, as well as this couple in my next brief story.

TEXAS 4 STEP

Eastbound rolling. I-10 just outside of Houston. Another batch of summer rain pounding the area. They say you're supposed to slow down in the rain. Some people don't know this apparently. They think they can drive the same in the rain as they do when the roads are dry.

Then they find out the hard way. Ooopps. Now they have a vehicle that's totaled, and they are in the hospital. They committed a "preventable" accident. A man driving, and his female companion in the passenger seat. Two lane highway, meaning two lanes eastbound, and two lanes westbound with another of those grass mediums in the middle. That seem to catch so many motorists every day. I'm in the far right lane, and people are passing me on the left. It's one of those miserable pouring rain days. This couple in a black pickup truck zoom past me, then start to spin out. First in their lane, then in my lane, then back into their lane.

Round and round he goes, where he stops, nobody knows. I could of T-boned the guy if I hadn't of been going about 55mph. My standard speed for rain. They managed to come to a stop in the, you guessed it, medium. Upright and shitting their pants, most likely. The female yelling at him. Seems to be the usual scene. But, wouldn't you rather not spin out and wind up in a accident?? Just curious.

THOSE DAMN ICY ROADS...

My first year driving. Scared half to death, driving on my first icy road. And it had to be in the Colorado Rockies of all places. Nice place to break you in. I am happy to report that I wasn't the only one scared that day. I had to leave Denver and go west on I-70, through the Rocky Mountains. The highest point through there on the road is around 11,000 feet. High enough. The road crew had not gotten to this area yet to plow it. Lay down the salt and shave the ice off the road. So we had to drive on it. Oh, and did I mention that I had about 42,000lbs load and there were areas that were 6% grade? Down hill? I got nervous going down a grade like that when the roads were nice and dry, let alone trying to make it down on the ice!

I wasn't the only one doing 15mph down the whole thing. I was just in the lead. I had about 4 other trucks behind me all feeling the same fear. We were white knuckling that baby. Talking back and forth on the cb. We managed to make it through the Rockies safe and sound and tired. I never mess around with slippery roads. And I don't care if I piss people off. You should of seen how some of the drivers where just zipping through there as though it was a race and the roads were dry. I thought that they must of just been really experienced. And maybe just a little stupid. Ok, 15mph is slow, but 50mph in the ice? I couldn't believe that. No way. Not me. I've got another ice story for you, if you want to hear it.

MISERY THANKS COMPANY

Christmas 2003. I have come to call the state of Missouri, Misery in the winter. It has been misery for me on several occasions. It's just the winter. I don't like the cold and snow and freezing temperatures. I always nag my boss for loads going south. This particular time going through the state, I was able to help some motorists out. Again, the roads were icy. I think that's why I call it misery. I don't see any snow plows clearing the roads. Not that they don't have any. I just haven't experienced them yet in the state. I'm driving west bound on another icy road when a mini van passes me on the left, then spins out.

This time, this spin out winds up crashing into the ditch on the right side of the road. They flipped their van. The driver of the van and his occupant where unhurt, thankfully. Just shook up quite a bit. It was freezing ass cold out there and I pulled over to help them. I let them stay in my warm truck until help arrived. I called 911 and gave them location and info.

A highway patrol officer arrived shortly after the crash and took care of them. I guessed that these were Mexicans. They couldn't speak very much English, and had the usual Mexican stickers on their vehicle. I know Mexicans from living in Los Angeles for most my life. Just as I was getting ready to pull away, here comes a little white pickup truck slipping and sliding all over the place. He eventually smashed the front of his pickup head on into the ditch. It was good that the officer helping the Mexicans was still there and he took care of the guy in the pickup truck as well. I pulled away and got the heck out of there. I drove slowly and carefully down the road.

Just a few more miles to go and I can call it a day. I had this one truck stop planned and was happily heading for it. Of course, on the way, I passed another accident scene. A guy pulling a utility trailer jackknifed and wound up in the right side ditch. I finally made it to the truck stop. The parking lot there hadn't been cleared up entirely, but there was a plow on a pickup working on it. With snow covering the ground, I could only take a calculated guess as to where the lot ended and the grassy ditch underneath began. I judged by a light pole about how much room I had. I began my backing in between two trucks and managed to make it perfectly without hitting them, or falling off the edge of the parking lot!! And it was a great parking spot too, right up front, close to the building. Warm meals, and a hot shower awaited me. Just another winter day in Misery.

ANIMALS I'VE SEEN

I've come across some really interesting animals in my travels. Being from Los Angeles, if I wanted to see some interesting species, I had to go to a zoo. I like seeing animals out in the wild. So far, I've seen a lot of deer and elk. I've seen Buffalo in Kansas and Wyoming, and saw a herd of Antelope in Wyoming. I saw a dead alligator in South Carolina. He must have been 10' long easily. His head was smashed and yellow stuff spilled out all over the ground. He lay on the side of the road, thankfully not out in the middle of the interstate.

Up in Maryland, West Virginia, and surrounding areas I've seen wild turkey grazing along the side of the road. Big birds. I think it's pretty cool to see that out the side of my window as I drive by. On my property in Florida, I saw two big vultures sitting on a fallen tree. They were huge, black and with red heads and red feet. I took a photo of them before they flew away. I've seen gophers, and otters. In Arizona I've seen road runners. They really are that fast. You can't run em' over if you tried.

They are actually a little bigger than you'd think. About the size of a big rat. In Arizona I've also seen big tarantulas crawling across the road. And scorpions, as well as snakes. Snakes go "pop" when you hit them. In Colorado I saw a bald eagle. He was flying right toward me and then turned away before he got too close. I saw his brown body and un-mistakenly white head. That was really cool. Another magical Colorado moment. I saw prairie dogs in Colorado too. They are cute and bark a lot. I've seen red foxes running near the road. And wolves, and coyotes.

In Florida I've seen many live gators while driving down Alligator Alley. Of course, you expect to see gators when driving on a road called Alligator Alley. I'd feel jipped if I didn't see at least one. But the best gator sight I saw was Nov 2004. I was on US Hwy 27, going north from Miami, through a rural area, to the Lakeland area. I saw a turnout for a mini rest area. As I was pulling into the rest area I saw a gator swimming in the channel that runs the entire length of the highway for many miles. I parked, grabbed my camera, and left my dog in the truck while I went to snap some photos of the gator. I walked over to the guard rail and the gator swam toward me. He stopped in the water about 50' from me and just watched me. He was checking me out. We sat there and stared at each other for about 10 minutes then he went under water. He popped up away from me on the other side of the canal.

I took more pictures, then took my dog for a walk. Keeping my eyes peeled for any more gators. I didn't see any more. Rowan smelled everything and left her doggy calling card in several places. Then we left. That was the coolest gator encounter I've ever had. On other occasions while driving next to water, I've seen beaver. With their distinctive tails. In Florida I've seen Great Blue Herons. They are big and pretty birds. Being from Los Angeles, these birds are exotic to me. You see a lot of white egret birds there too. And I've seen these egrets in California too. Around the Sacramento area. Along the I-5 corridor. I've seen dolphins while driving on I-95 northbound in Georgia. They are black dolphins. I am sure I am not mistaken. It wasn't the clouds, or color of the water. They swim up in the rivers from the ocean. I always look for them when I'm on I-95 going north in Georgia, from the Florida border until there is no water anymore on the side of the road.

I got a kick out of seeing my first Canadian Geese flying and squawking while they fly. I'd be in the Chicago area going to or from a customer and see them grazing in a patch of grass. Here, in the middle of a busy city, traffic buzzing all around. Big buildings all over. And these geese are just making themselves at home. Many people don't like these geese, especially those that take care of golf courses. And golfers too. Because of all the geese poop. And for that matter, any sporting place where there is grass. Like baseball diamonds, football fields, and parks. Try playing a little light tackle football and wind up falling in a pile of geese poop! Otherwise, I like them. As long as they aren't pooping in my place. I saw a wild pig in Florida when I was pulling into a inspection station. I told the officer and he replied that the pig is their mascot.

That he just comes and goes as he pleases and doesn't bother anyone. I'm worried about him getting ran over. The officer said he's smart and stays away from the traffic. Once when I was pulling out of a weigh station in Florida, I actually put my 4way flashers on, stopped my truck, got out, and grabbed a big turtle out of the road before he got ran over. I put him back in the bushes way off the side of the road. I don't like seeing animals get run over.

One day when I was driving southbound on the I-15 from Utah to Las Vegas, I passed through the small bit of Arizona, and through the Virgin River Gorge. If you keep your eyes open, but careful to watch the road as well, you may see some bighorn sheep grazing by the road. I saw about 5-6 bighorn sheep and I was able to pull over, off the road into a big dirt area and take some pictures. I wasn't the only one pulled over too. Fellow travelers and I cautiously crept as close to the animals as we dare. It was a fun and exciting encounter.

MY SILLY DOG & THE COP
I have a 4yr old Chow-Shepherd mix girl dog named Rowan. She has the intelligence of the shepherd, and the cutest little face in my opinion. She loves to play in the snow a lot. I take her out to pee, and she plays instead. Like a kid. One evening when I was in a small Georgia town looking for a customer that had moved to a new location, Rowan did something unbelievable. There were two police cars parked nearby talking to each other. I was out walking Rowan and approached them.

They were friendly and helpful. One officer was a dog lover and reached through his open window to pet her. I told her to get "up" on his window sill so he could reach her better. Since she is a trucker dog and used to jumping way up into the cab, she thought that's what I meant. She promptly jumped "up" and into the officers window and landed in his lap! I was so embarrassed. She was sitting between the steering wheel and his chest. And she's not exactly a small dog. She's about 50lbs and medium size.

The officer didn't seem to mind and he laughed a bit. I was so sorry. I kept apologizing to him. She loves to play with people and is especially affectionate towards men as she was raised by men before I got her, at 6 months old. They loved and spoiled her, and would cuddle with her when she was a baby. We both managed to get Rowan off him and back outside his car. I didn't punish my girl for doing that. She was doing what she was told.

I always tell her "up" to get her in the truck. She likes to stall and take her time. She'd rather be outside the truck and playing. I don't blame her. Me too! But we have a job to do, and a mortgage to pay. I do give her every opportunity to run and play and she knows this country well. Place by place, smell by smell. This was by far her most amazing little trick yet! There's one nice cop in a small town in Georgia that won't soon forget her.

STRANGE THINGS IN THE SKY

On one dark and lonely night, pulling a all-nighter, I was driving in Arizona and saw something strange. I hate these drive all night with no sleep loads. I try not to take them. I was very tired. Trying everything to stay awake. Keeping my eyes barely open, I saw a fireball come down to earth, same direction as I was traveling. So big. Huge ball of fire. I thought for sure it was a meteorite and that I would witness it crash to earth in a big ball of fire. And set ablaze acres of desert grass for miles. It was not far from the left side of the highway. I kept my eyes peeled, looking for the fallen fireball. I thought since it was so close to the highway that I would surely see it close to the road.

How can you miss a huge fireball?? Well, I looked and looked, I slowed down, I was the only vehicle around for miles. Kept looking for it, and never saw it. I thought for sure I'd hear something about it on the news, but never did. Maybe this thing happens a lot in the Arizona desert.

Sept 15, 2001 IOWA. I pulled over late one night at a weigh station not far from my delivery the next morning. I was one of two big trucks parked there. This location was out in the middle of nowhere. It was not long after the Sept 11 attacks that were fresh on everyone's minds, including mine. I'm was sleeping away when I heard what sounded like an airplane going to land on my truck! The sound was faint at first, then got louder, and louder, and LOUDER!! It was for sure, I thought. I know something is going to land right on my truck. I jumped out of bed and look out the window and saw a helicopter landing in front of my truck, about 50' from me. He was landing on a helipad, and parked in front of my truck was an ambulance. I thought "What the hell is going on?". I thought that maybe the driver in the truck next to me was having a heart attack or something.

And he was able to call 911 before he passed out or something. But then a police officer also on the scene walked up to my window. I rolled it down and she said "They are transporting a little boy via helicopter to the hospital, he's having a asthma attack". Oh, I said. I know what that's like as far as one of my sister's is concerned. She would have a bad attack in the middle of the night and had to be rushed to the hospital. I told the officer that I hoped he'll be ok, and she assured me he will. Then the copter noisily took off and the ambulance and police left and that was it. There is nothing like the sound of a helicopter landing 50' from you at night when you are in a little sleeper cab fast asleep. Scared the crap out of me for a minute or two.

IS X-FILES REAL??

I'd like to start out by saying that I wasn't the only one that saw them that day. How could you miss them? Driving eastbound on the I-40 in New Mexico trying to be low key. About 3 big rigs, plain wrap, gray color convoy. Government plates. The drivers all wearing the same type of sunglasses, and dressed the same. These big rigs were escorted by about 2 vans per truck, plain colors. Also Government plates. The drivers of the vans dressed like FBI agents, and all wearing the same sunglasses. The chatter on the cb was "What could they be hauling?". They were headed in the direction of Area 51. Catch the US Hwy 285 south and they'd be there by nightfall. Hhhmmmmm???

HURRICANE RELIEF

Summer 2004. Four Hurricanes hit Florida in one season. Charley, Ivan, Frances, and Jeanne. I have land near Gainesville and only have a little motor home sitting on it. No power or utilities yet. I call my little rv, the little winne that stood. It stayed upright throughout the entire hurricane season. I only lost a big oak tree that crashed on my neighbor's fence. My neighbor used his friend and chain saws to cut it all up and use it for firewood.

I figure that my location had something to do with not being hit "too bad" by the hurricanes. I'm up in the northern, middle part of the state. By the time the hurricanes' make their way up there, they have been traveling over 300 miles on land, which slows them down. I was counting on that. All 4 times! I was able to help with hurricane relief during the 2004 season. I got loads of water and tarps and delivered them to the much needed areas. I was happy to help in my small way.

TRUCK MECHANICAL PROBLEMS

Nothing is more unnerving than having your battery box break on you during a trip. These battery boxes hold 4 big truck batteries. The weld broke and the box wedged at a angle on it's support frame. I was afraid of sparks and fire. I tried to tie up the box as best I could so it wouldn't fall any further. Yikes!! I had to drive over 200 miles with a broken battery box. How about a good oil leak? When it happens to a big rig, it happens in it's own unique big way. I had a valve cover gasket blow on me which spewed gallons of oil over the entire rear portion of my truck, and front of the trailer.

What a huge mess. I managed to make it to a truck dealer and they fixed it in a day. But, prior to my bringing the injured truck in, I put my one and only gallon of spare oil in the engine. Bringing the gauge up to ¼ full. After they spent all day fixing the gasket, they released me and sent me on my way. Before I left, I asked them if they put any oil in it? They had this look on their faces that told the answer. Ooopps! We forgot that. Jeez, after all that, they would send me out with NO OIL in my engine?? At least no oil registering on the dipstick???!!! I managed to wrangle a free gallon out of them, then I went on my way!!

How about a rough running engine? These big rigs are not indestructible, as they may seem to be. On one particular day, I noticed my truck coughing and running really bad. It was losing power getting up highway onramps. It would run rough at a cruising speed of 60-65mph. I got the truck into the shop and found that it was a fuel injector that had gone bad. I got to spend a whole week in a hotel room with my dog while I waited for the repair. The cost of the hotel was paid by the company I work for, as well as I got $50 a day for being stuck waiting for repairs. I figure, that's all better than nothing. While staying in the hotel with cable tv, I got addicted to home repair and garden shows. And I enjoy the travel shows too.

HEROES OF THE HIGHWAY

Truckers were once known to be heroes of the highway. Whenever a motorist broke down or had a accident, truckers would always help. It's the same way now. We pride ourselves on helping motorists in need. And the trucking industry recognizes them. The following is one such story of a trucker reaching out to help a motorist in need. And there are many more stories like this out there.

Trucker Credited with Saving Lives of Three:
Little Rock, Ark.
Trucker Mike McMann sacrificed his new Peterbuilt tractor and his own life on one fateful winter morning in Arkansas. The lives of three others were on the line. Joe Clifford of Olive Branch, Mississippi, said McMann put the lives of his family ahead of his own in the aftermath of a winter storm on I-30, just west of Little Rock. In a report the motorist stated that the driver of the Big Rig may have saved his life and the lives of his family by risking his own life to prevent serious injury or death to his family. Joe, his wife, and daughter were driving the family's Ford Explorer west on I-30 to Texas to spend time with family over the holidays. The roads were covered with ice from the storm the night before. As is the custom of Arkansas, the roads are not usually cleared for such a condition.

The state does not keep the necessary snow plows and salting trucks for snow and ice storms. So motorists must drive on ice during those times. As Joe and his family were making a lane change to exit the highway, he began sliding. Fishtailing from side to side, and then spinning completely around several times. They spun into the center of the road hitting the concrete wall head-on.

Joe's vehicle came to a stop sideways to the oncoming traffic. Joe remembers seeing the semi heading straight for him and realized in an instant that the truck "can't stop" in time. When Joe regained consciousness a short time later in the hospital, he was told of what the trucker had done. The driver of the Peterbuilt had intentionally hit the concrete barrier to slow himself down as much as possible before hitting Joe and his family. Thanks largely to his quick thinking, Joe and his family only sustained minor injuries. Joe and his family were wearing their seatbelts at the time and give credit to the seatbelts also helping to save their lives. As for the truck driver, his truck did suffer some minor repairable damage.

Truck driver Mike McMann stopped to check on Joe and his family and called for help. The Clifford's stated in the report that they would like to publicly thank the truck driver for doing his best to prevent death or serious injury.

TRUCKER BUDDY PROGRAM

Trucker Buddy International. www.truckerbuddy.org
This is a non-profit organization dedicated to helping educate and mentor school children. Trucker Buddy matches classes of students with professional truck drivers. Once a week drivers share news of their travels with their class. Once a month students write letters to their drivers. Since 1992, Trucker Buddy has helped educate over 500,000 schoolchildren and introduced them to caring, compassionate men and women, professional truck drivers. 1-800-MY-BUDDY

BEST AND WORST STATES FOR DRIVING. One of the absolute worst states to drive in is Texas. The road designs are mostly ridiculous. After you've driven for over 400 miles of drop dead boring nothingness, you get to a city or town and that's where the trouble starts. Some of the on and off ramps are literally tight S's. If you don't slow down you will surely flip your car, truck, or suv. And when you make it through that, watch out for on-coming traffic. The frontage roads running along the sides of most of the big highways are two way. Most of them are this way.

And one other thing to note when you are driving in Texas: U-TURNS. You can actually see where you want to go, but will have to go through an idiotic maze of loops, spurs, and u-turns before you can actually get to the place you want. You can see it, but you can't get to it. Or so it feels. You get pissed off after an hour of trying. The key is to get off on the exit BEFORE the one you want and take the frontage roads then do a u-turn and you should be able to get there. Dallas is one of the worst cities to drive in the entire lower 48 states. They call it the mix-master. It's more like a child with a crayon drawing haphazardly designed the freeway systems in that city. You can see where they tried to make improvements, but in my opinion only made it worse.

If you have enough notice ahead of time, instead of at the last minute, you can suddenly race across four lanes of high speed traffic to get to your exit. Or, it might be on the other side of the road. A left exit. Whatever floats the engineers and designers fancy at the time. Some of the roads are newly paved and are pretty smooth.

But many of them will loosen the fillings in your teeth and cause you to lose several car parts before reaching your destination. But one nice thing I can say about Texas is, they have interesting architectural restaurant designs. They seem to go all out in building their eating establishments. And the food in Texas is great. That is, once you can dart across traffic and make several u-turns and finally get to the restaurant. Then, have a beer or margarita, stuff yourself with steak and potatoes and you'll forget all about the roads and driving hassles.

Arkansas does not do winter storms well at all. In my opinion it shouldn't matter that it snows maybe once a year and the roads get covered with ice for about a week. They do not seem to have snowplows or salt trucks. Sure, they'll throw some dirt on it and I guess we should be grateful for at least *that* much. I'm surprised that the state has not been sued by a class-action lawsuits by all the motorists that slid off their icy roads and crashed. Holding the state of Arkansas responsible for not cleaning their roads as best they can during snow and ice storms. They just expect people to drive on it. In other states, when the roads get that bad, they either close the roads or require chains. Not Arkansas. We should try and get ol' Bill Clinton to fork over some of his millions to buy his state some multi-use dump truck-salt-snow plow type vehicles. Other states attack the roads before the first snow flakes hit the ground. Not Arkansas. You may even slide into and run over the many State Troopers by the side of the road helping those unfortunate enough to be in the state at the time, that had slid off into a ditch or into each other.

And when it's not sliding around on ice, it's going over bumpy roads that literally make you feel like you are riding a damn bucking bronco bull. For miles and miles this goes on. You are almost ready for the hospital with back and neck injuries by the time you make it out of the state. Yes, I know they have made some road improvements. But let's get ol' Bill Clinton to fork over some dough so they can bring their state's roads up to par with many others in the country. Other than the bone rattling, and sometimes icy roads, Arkansas is a beautiful state.

THE BEST STATE that I can think of at this time is MARYLAND. They have good, clean of ice roads (during winter) and noticeably big and plentiful signage. They post road and street signs everywhere. You should not get lost in Maryland. At every junction, there are signs. Which way to go. This route, that Interstate, etc.. And Maryland has a lot of traffic lights and intersection stop signs. They want to make sure that motorists can actually pull out into traffic lanes and not be run over by someone buzzing by exceeding the speed limit.

In some states, rural areas mostly. They do not have their act together. I mean having sense enough to put a traffic light or at least some stop signs at interstate on and off ramps. So that you can get into your intended traffic lanes, or at least pull out of a shopping center without getting crashed into by the many people that blatantly ignore the speed limits. Some states must think that people can see a tiny sign, 200' away, on some far corner of the intersection and be able to tell whether or not that is the street in which they need to turn on! I mean really, some places you need binoculars to read a damn street sign.

And that's even if there *is* a sign in the first place!! My advice, begging, pleading to DEPT OF ROADS AND SIGNS IN ALL STATES IS: Please make road signs BIG AND EASY TO READ. And place them AT ALL CORNERS of the intersections to that we can see them. THANK YOU!!!! And PLEASE MAKE STOP SIGNS AT ALL CORNERS OF INTERSECTIONS!!

Unless there is a traffic light that you somehow managed to wrangle out of the tight ass government running your state. It might actually cut down on the number of traffic accidents. Imagine that. I would also like to add that there are states in this huge and wonderful country of ours that do a great job in attacking, plowing, salting, and maintaining clean and ice free roads for us to drive on. And I, as well as most motorists, do appreciate your hard work and efforts. The money you spend to make sure your roads are clean, smooth and safe, is worth it. And it should pay off in less traffic accidents and fatalities. Thank you for your work. And keep pushing for those roads funds. We all need them if we are to live and drive in your state.

BEST & WORST DRIVERS by CITY: As in most large cities, we all find rude and aggressive drivers. They speed up and cut you off and won't let you over when you have your blinker on. Or cut in front of you at the last minute when they're merging lane is running out, and all the stupid things they do. This is a problem in all cities in our lower 48 states that I have been in. What stands out to me about the BEST DRIVERS is that they let you over when you have your blinker on, and mostly do the posted speed limits. The two places that top the list, that *are* the list are: Maryland & Sacramento, Calif.

There have been several times I have been stuck in morning commuter traffic in Sacramento, Calif. One thing that I noticed stood out was that when I had my blinker on, the motorists' actually let me over. Some even flashed their headlights to signal ok to get over. I would flash my lights in a "thank you" gesture. It is not common in any city in America that people actually let you over when you need to get over. I was impressed by the drivers' in Sacramento, Calif. and appreciate the courtesy. In the State of Maryland, I have noticed a big difference in the drivers' that actually do the speed limit and again, let you over when you have your blinker on. Part of this has to do with the "Aggressive Driver Imaging" System they have in many locations throughout their state. It seems to be working from this outsider's point of view. It's big enough to be noticeable.

To all the drivers' of all the types of vehicles out there in America, that *do* drive the speed limit and *are* courteous to other motorists on the road, THANK YOU, and keep up the good driving. We NEED more drivers like you.

CHAPTER 7
HOLLYWOOD INFO
Living and working in Hollywood, Celebrity Encounters; Chuck Norris, Robert Urich,
Kevin Bacon, Charlie Sheen, Dustin Hoffman and more.

In my early 20's after I saw Mel Gibson's movie "The Road Warrior", I was fascinated by
stunts. Growing up in the South Bay, Calif, it was not too far a drive to Hollywood. At that
time I was heavily into karate, surfing, motorcycles, skateboarding, and car stunts. Or more
like "car thrashing". I tried out for stunt jobs on Baywatch, Batman with Michael Keaton,
and every show I could get to when I wasn't working full time. I signed up with Joni's Stunt
People, and tried to surround myself with as many stunt people in the business as I could. I
had pictures made (called "headshots") and tried hard to break into the stunt business.

I was young and very athletic and ambitious. It's a very difficult business to get into. After all
my failed attempts, I went back to working in a office. I hated it. The people drove me up
the wall with their stupid antics and comments. I was a little discouraged. I wrote some short
stories and screenplays, went to college and studied business and kept dragging on. Many
years later, I tried Hollywood again. This time from a different angle. I focused on Props and
Art Dept. I got a lot closer doing this work than trying stunt work.

In order for this new plan to work, I had to adjust my living environment. Actually, I had to
move out of my apartment due to rapid increase in rent by new owners. So I lived in a van
for awhile. I bought the van from an unknown actor. He put the words "For Sale" on the
back of a resume and taped the sign in the window. The extremely ugly van cost me $400
and barely ran. The transmission had a bad habit of slamming into gear so hard, it would
give you whiplash.

But it was within my miniscule budget so I bought it. I lived on savings for a few months
while trying again to "break in" to Hollywood. This van had a smashed front end and was
so ugly, that friends and family didn't want me to park it near their homes. It had a kitchen
and bathroom and a mattress. That's all I needed. My boxer dog Brandy and I made it into
the best home we could until I moved my life in yet another direction. It was actually not
bad living like that. I just parked in a different place each night, in good neighborhoods and
even worked part time in a big book store to earn some living cash. I belonged to a gym and
would work out then shower afterwards.

At times I would park at the beach and enjoy my free ocean view, while people in the high
priced condos near me where paying through the nose! I had everything I needed; a place to
sleep, and bathroom, and I kept warm and dry. I read a lot of books and wrote a lot too.
During this time in the van, I was able to get intern work on a few productions. I found
them in the trades (trades are the Hollywood Reporter and The Daily Variety newspapers
you can find at 7-11 stores and many other bookstores and newsstands).

And I also went to American Film Institute on Western Ave in Hollywood. I would check AFI's bulletin boards for help wanted. Internship does not pay money. But you get free food on the sets' , experience, and networking with people in the business, and you have a lot of fun. Many people I found that were making their films were already established in the industry and were looking to become directors. On one such project I worked as Prop Master. It was very helpful to have a van to haul stuff. Even if it was extremely ugly. The person in charge of the Art Dept worked at Paramount Pictures. She took myself and others in the Art Dept to the studios to load up on props. It was a really cool experience. You see known actors walking around in costume and smile at them. I try to be cool and nonchalant. Like, I see big stars every day! These prop rooms are very exciting and often several levels inside.

You see stuff that you've seen in movies. I was excited. Every item no matter how big or small is cataloged and inventoried. So we would just walk the rows looking for what we need and fill our carts and baskets. As we were working, a group of tourists following their guide strolled by and stopped to listen to the guide. We smiled and waved at the tourists. And then they moved on to other parts of the studio. Outside sat my ugly van and we loaded it up. Some people openly wondered "Does that thing run?". Once fully loaded, we leave. Waving goodbye to the guard as my ugly van exits on one side, and big stars enter on the other side of the guard shack.

Somewhere in the middle of downtown Hollywood, during rush hour traffic which is always rush hour, my transmission goes out. One last SLAM! And whiplash for good measure, then die. No forward, no backward. Right in the middle of a turn lane. Cars are honking at me as if I'm insane to have my van die right there. I yell back at them that "You think I'm doing this on purpose you idiot? I would move it if I could you stupid jerk". They get all pissed off and throw tantrum fits then manage to get around me. I call the director. She is extremely sweet and comes to rescue me, bringing along the producer. I am so sorry, I tell them. I'm near tears.

They help me push the van out of traffic and we begin to transfer all the props into their cars. They tell me it's ok and not to worry. I'm still so sorry, I tell them. They are very sweet and handle the fiasco well, and wind up buying me lunch. I get my van towed to a shop and it costs me $350 for a rebuilt tranny. A week later, I'm back on the road, having stayed with friends while my van was being repaired. One day, the producer, director, some of the actors and other production staff went to a film lab to look at some test film. They were deciding how they want the film color, editing, etc.. to look.

I got to go along and watch this process. It was interesting. This lab can take film and transfer it to video at different qualities and options. Afterward, the producer needed a ride into Hollywood to get some filming permits. I wound up being the only person available to give him a ride. No problem I say. Glad to help. But my ugly van has only one seat. Mine. There is no passenger seat or seats in the back. Just my mattress. So he cautiously gets in and sits on my bed. My dog brandy loves licking people in the face and promptly made herself friendly with him. So we leave Burbank and take a road with a lot of curves and hills to get down to Hollywood and the permits office.

This nice, clean producer is thrown around in my van. Tossed all over. He tries to find something to hold on to, and only finds my dog right there, in his face. He's being tossed around and licked. Brandy stands firm like a surfer. She's got good footing and is used to this. The producer keeps gently trying to push Brandy away from him. Oh, and did I mention it was summer and about 100 degrees in the van with no air conditioning? We finally get there and the nice, clean producer exits looking relieved, sweaty, and rumpled. He's just had the hell ride of his life. I offer to take him anywhere else he needs to go, and he politely declines. Stating someone is due to met him there and they will ride together. Most likely in a vehicle with seats, no dog, and air conditioning!

I did a few more intern jobs but couldn't get a paying film job. So I had to go back to a real job. I worked in a big bookstore wherehouse. I kept getting in trouble for reading the incoming books as I was sorting them. I couldn't help it. They were/are so interesting. I practically would spend most of my paychecks on books. I had to get out of there and get a different job! After the bookstore job, I went to truck driving school for a month. Trying to break into the Hollywood film business was too hard for me. I did learn many lessons that I would be happy to pass on to those that may want to try their luck in Hollywood. There are a lot of scams out there. Anytime people ask for a fee up front, FOR ANYTHING, don't go for it. Decline. A real Hollywood agent will make his/her money from real acting/working jobs. And nowadays with computers the way they are, you can make and print your own headshots (photos of your cute face) with your (padded, I recommend at first) resume printed on a page attached to the back.

Who's gonna check if your resume is padded? By padded I mean, add on some extra work you may not have done, but can be hidden in the largeness of the film or show. It's ok. Many people do it!! Hee hee. I'm sure this is obvious, but get as many books as you can on acting and Hollywood. Which I'm sure you already are doing. You are building your library. When you get to Hollywood, you may be in for a culture shock. The city moves super fast. The people wear black mostly. And everybody's got a script or something they are working on. There is no shortage of fellow actors, writers, directors, etc.. in the city. Stop in and see as many plays as you like. Small playhouses dot the city landscape and offer unique, offbeat, and funny shows. If you don't want to live in a van, you can go for the roommate setup.

You may go through several before you find one that 1) won't stiff you on rent, 2) won't run your phone bill up and not pay, 3) won't get you to pay for all the food and 4) won't hustle you into driving them places with promises to pay for gas once you get there. Then give world class excuses why they can't pay for gas. Gee, I coulda seen that one coming! Once you finally find a decent roommate, you can get some serious work done. You'll most likely work at least 2 jobs minimum. That's so you can pay all your rent, food, insurance, etc... This is typical of L.A., low pay and high cost of living. Better be as prepared for it as possible. Save your money at every opportunity.

You'll be surprised as to how many people have car problems in L.A. That's so you can be hustled into giving them a ride. Too bad you're car doesn't work. Take a bus or walk then. Watch out for these clever hustlers. They are everywhere. But, not to be too down on the place, I actually know quite a few really nice, decent, and good people in Hollywood. It's possible to find people like that there. But, you will have your share of b.s. people you will have to deal with, work with, and encounter. It comes with the territory. Don't be too trusting. Be careful. Watch your back. Don't loan money or anything for any reason. No matter their oscar winning performance show they will put on. Begging, whining, practically crying on you. DON'T LOAN ANYTHING.

And you'll be a lot better off. You must set the standard or you can be walked all over and taken full advantage of. A good response is: "Sorry, I can't loan you any money, I'm broke. Just like everybody else". or "Sorry, I can't give you a ride, my car is not running good. I think it's a injector problem, or transmission problem". You may start out wanting a nice car in L.A. People do judge you by what you drive out there. I always just shunned that, but that's me. I never cared what they thought. Heck, I couldn't afford much more than I had anyway. But, people do keep up with appearances. Be careful not to get a popular car that is a target to be stolen.

May I suggest getting yourself a beater car? Older, some dents. Not very attractive, but must run great. That way, when you get dents on it, which will happen, you don't worry that much about it. And you're car will be there, when newer, fancier cars will be stolen. I call a beat up old car, but runs good, a perfect L.A. car. You'll need car insurance, it's the law, and smog check. Most gas stations have the smog check thing going on. You'll have to get it smogged and insured before you can get it registered. Make sure you have a clear title (or pink slip, they call it).

Otherwise, you may be buying a stolen car. Make sure the vin # on the title matches the vin# on the car. You would be surprised the scams that happen in Calif. Especially to a supposedly innocent and naïve out of stater. Again, I'm not out to bash L.A., thankfully, there are good places to do car business. Honest people. Most people can recommend a good mechanic or car place. They have been through a lot already. Another thing to watch out for when buying a car, is a title that says "salvage" on it. The seller will give you all kinds of lies. He'll say he lost the title and this is a replacement. No matter what he says, the true meaning of salvage title is that this vehicle has been badly damaged in a accident.

And the insurance company wrote it off. Sellers buy these cars at public auction for cheap, may fix them up a bit, then sell for profit to un-suspecting buyers. You may notice frame damage if you drive behind the car and it dog tracks, goes sideways down the road. That's major frame damage my friend. Stay away from that car. Politely decline. When looking to buy a car, take a magnet, any magnet will do, from your refrigerator or somewhere. Take the magnet and run it all along the car on all metal parts all over it. If the magnet doesn't stick, there is bondo there. Meaning the car has had major repairs that the seller is not disclosing to you.

Some bondo has metal flakes put in it so it's harder to detect. Knock the panels with your knuckle and listen for a sound differation. Also, one more important note. Make sure the title is in the seller's name before you buy. He/she may give more world class lies and excuses, but the real reason is they want to sell the car and make a profit and not pay taxes on that profit. That's why they don't put it in their name. Check their I.D.'s too. Tell them it's not personal, just business. They will act all offended at this request. But, if they don't have anything to hide, it shouldn't be a problem.

These are just a few of the common scams that are very prevalent in L.A. For the most part, you can't expect people to be honest and decent. They have to scam in order to survive. That's how they see it. Like it or not, that is the truth you will find out in L.A. Not everyone is like that. There are some good folks out there. But you will have to do some careful looking to find the good ones. Having been born and raised in the L.A. area, I have plenty of experience to share. And I have over 10 years experience in the car business. From shops, to parts, to sales, to bookkeeping, to overseas shipping. I've been around. When driving the vehicle, make sure the transmission shifts smoothly. If it slams into gear, don't buy it.

That slamming means it's going to fail soon and most likely when you are in traffic. Don't believe anything the seller says about it either. They will lie in order to sell the car. Just say, no thanks, and walk away. Don't be afraid to be rude. Be firm. Hold your ground. Sellers' may be very pushy and aggressive. Don't be afraid to be rude and walk away. And one more thing, you may find that some people in L.A. will try to blind side you. In other words, hustle you into paying for their meal when you all go out to eat. An idiot that tries to get you to pay for them is not a friend. When the bill comes due and they give excuses that they can't pay. They left their wallet or something….too bad. Tough shit.

YOU are not responsible to pay their meal bill. Tell the management that you will not pay for anyone other than yourself. Let that idiot wash dishes to pay for his/her meal. People try this shit all the time. They try to blind side you into paying for them. Stand your ground. Hold your own. When they realize that they can't take advantage of you, they will move on to someone that is easier to hustle. You'll survive the drama and the ordeal that this idiot will put you through. You pay your meal bill, and leave. Always drive your own car so you can be in control of when you come and go. Just tell people that you will meet them there. That way, you're not stuck getting a ride from the idiot that tries to make you pay their meal bill. Again, don't let yourself be blindsided by them.

They will try. Because it's hard to survive in L.A. People are barely getting by. Can hardly afford to eat, let alone pay rent, gas, car payments, and high credit card bills. They are maxed out, stretched thin. So you will find a lot of hustlers out there. Watch your ass.

CELEBRITY ENCOUNTERS
Charlie Sheen, Chuck Norris, Robert Urich,
Dustin Hoffman, Kevin Bacon, Roy Rogers and
his wife Dale Evans.

Now for the fun part. You may find yourself meeting the occasional celebrity in L.A. They live and work there. For the most part. When you see a celebrity, be cool. Don't ever bother them when they are eating. It's rude. Timing is important when asking for a photo or autograph. Be very polite and respectful to them. Don't' be too aggressive or irritate them. California has the strictest laws when it comes to celebrity stalking. You can easily find yourself arrested, thrown in jail, and humiliated on public television. You best be careful when you approach a celebrity. They can be very protective of themselves, as well as those people that are with them, can be very protective of them as well.

And for good and obvious reasons. We care about their safety and well being. With that said, I will now share some of my celebrity encounters with you. My first celebrity encounter was in the summer of 1979 in Maui, Hawaii. I had won a one week all expenses paid trip to Maui through our local newspaper. Where I was employed as a paper carrier. At age 14, I delivered to subscribers via bicycle and moped. Since we were young teens, we had several chaperones. My female roommates at The Whaler Condos where we all were staying, first noticed this Big Movie Star. They pointed him out to me, the brave and adventurous one.

At the time, I looked like a drowned rat. Having just come in from skin diving. I approached him in the little lobby store. As I got closer I smiled to him and said hi and introduced myself. He smiled back and said hi, and we shook hands. I was a very brave and bold kid and asked if I could take a photo of him. He smiled and said yes. But, I said, my camera is in my room, and asked if he would wait for me while I ran to get it. Actor Dustin Hoffman smiled sweetly and agreed to wait for me. Me, this ratty looking, sopping wet kid. I ran like the wind and was back in a flash. He was still there, looking at magazines. He had waited for me. What a nice guy. And, silly me, doing what my family has done for years, asked him to go outside for the photo. For a good background.

We always moved our photo group so we can have a good background. Then my mom would take a photo, cutting off our heads in the picture!! Who is this headless family? Thankfully, other family members took photos too. So we managed to have some decent pictures to keep. So, here I am, a 14yr old tomboy, looking disheveled, standing there with Actor Dustin Hoffman, and asking him "Mr. Hoffman, can you please move over here so this solid color wall is behind you?". For a good background!! He was very sweet and patient with this kid, me. I snapped the photo, getting a good picture. Of all of him. Head and all. And shook his hand again and thanked him.

I was really nervous and was trying to be as cool as possible. The photo came out good. He was smiling and holding a tennis racket and some books. I saw him again later on that day playing tennis, and took a few more pictures of him. Thanks again, Mr. Hoffman.

CHUCK NORRIS: I met Mr.Norris for the first time of many at the karate studio where I trained. In Torrance, Ca. It was in the 1980's. My Instructor was one of his stuntmen. Mr.Norris signed a autograph for me and took a photo with me. He was very nice and polite. It was during the time when he lived near me. Torrance is close to Rolling Hills Estates. Sometimes my friends and I would cruise past his nice big house. And on occasion would see his Mercedes with "Top Kick" on the license plate. I would never be disrespectful and approach his home and knock on the door. I would never bother him. Nor would I ever leave a letter or note for him.

That would obviously be pushing it too far and be invasion of his privacy. His sons attended high school at the same time I did. Our schools would sometimes play football against each other. I would be on the West High band pep squad as a drummer. We would watch the game and see his oldest son playing. We also saw that Mr.Norris made time to watch his children playing sports. He was not too busy to come to a game or two. Mr.Norris also graduated from North High School in Torrance, Ca. To us, he's a "local boy done good". As his professional career took off and became very successful. We have a sense of pride when it comes to Chuck Norris.

During the promotion of his movie "Lone Wolf McQuade", our karate school put on a stunt and karate demonstration at the local Del Amo Mall in Torrance, Ca. This was one of the funest experiences I've ever had. I took a lot of photos of stunt men dressed as ninjas' decending from the ceiling to the ground. Ninja's and stuntmen fighting and falling over the railing on the second floor to land on boxes and cushions on the first level floor. It was a huge demo. Mr. Norris and L.A. Dodger baseball player Steve Sax were there. Mr. Sax trained with my instructor. Both Mr.Sax and Mr.Norris signed autographs.

I got to help with crowd control. I stood next to Mr.Norris and allowed only one person at a time to approach his table. And I would fetch a bottle of water for them from time to time. It felt like a honor to me to be there, and be able to help and participate in any little way I could. I was super excited and most likely a little hyper that day. A little more than usual. Not only did I love stunts at the time, but to be near Mr.Norris was so very exciting. I still love stunts, and Jackie Chan is by far my most favorite stunt performer. He is amazing. His physical strength and athletic ness. And creativity. It was fun to be a part of the demo and see how Mr.Norris's fans' reacted to him. They were lined up all over the mall. Winding here and there. Some women were nervous, giggly and giving him hugs. There was a energy in the air. Mr. Norris was genuine, kind, sweet and gracious.

As he left to go home, he shook all the participants hands, including mine. He was nice to everyone, even the "little people" like me. I took a lot a photos that day and still have them. I started karate at age 18 at Chuck Norris Karate in Torrance, Ca. Neat Gable House Bowl. I have photos and t-shirts from that time, still. And some newspapers write-ups about Mr.Norris back then as well.

His karate at the time was called U.F.A.F. United Fighting Arts Federation. I still have the old uniforms with the patches on them, and the t-shirts. I am a avid collector of just about everything! Back then, I was very hyperactive, young, filled with raging hormones over the cute guys working out with or without their t-shirts on!! I had a abundance of energy which karate was a good outlet.

Punching, kicking, sparring, and so on. My instructors will tell you that I was practically bouncing off the walls and ceilings. I had too much energy. I stayed with karate on and off for approx 15 years, eventually earning my black belt with a different karate school. I taught for a short time as well. I will always love karate. It is in my blood. I need to get back to working out. I'm a lot older now, and out of shape. I vow to get back to training as soon as I can. After I get a home for myself on my property in Florida. Then I won't have to drive a semi all over the country. I can actually take a local job and be home on a regular basis. I do sit ups and leg lifts in my truck, and walk a lot. But that's not enough. I need more.

EMELIO ESTEVEZ: March 1989. Redondo Beach, Ca. I was staying with my two older pain in the butt brothers in a apartment a few blocks from the beach. I noticed a movie being filmed down by the beach so I went to investigate. It was "Men at Work" with Emelio Estevez and his brother Charlie Sheen. I saw them both, but only talked to only Emelio. As we were making small talk, I petted his cute dog. I was shy and a bit self-conscious of what I was wearing. I had ridden my skateboard down there and was sporting the skater look. Only a girl could get away with wearing bright pink sweat pants with a surf co. logo running down one leg. And my sweatshirt was black with a skate co. logo on the back and little white bats running up and down on each long sleeve.

I must have been a odd sight. Emelio didn't seem at all phased by my appearance. Not bothered at all. He was very cool and casual. Polite and friendly. There were two young girls standing next to me that had run home and got themselves all dolled up. Trying to look as sexy as they could. They flirted with Emelio. He was polite and chatted with them a bit then went back to work. The babes eventually left and I stayed till 1am. I was waiting for a car stunt. They were running a car down the alley and a big yellow barrel would fall out of the trunk. I was hoping that the car would flip over or something. They would do this stunt over and over again. I was standing on one side of the alley, and Emelio was standing directly across from me. He kept looking my way and smiling.

I would smile shyly back at him. No one seemed to be bothered by me being there, watching the action. I stayed and watched for awhile and left when my shyness go to be too much for me. Emelio was very nice and handsome. I just couldn't hang in there any longer. I was too shy to stay. So much for the brave and bold one I used to be! It was many years later that I met his brother Charlie Sheen up close. I was working at a car lot in Redondo Beach. I was the only one besides the owner that was actually a licensed car salesperson. Of which, in California, you had to have all your fingers printed at the dmv to get your license. Hmmmm, I wonder why some sales people don't want to be licensed??? Hmmmm?

Anywho, I was just sitting there passing the time when two men walked on the lot. It was getting close to closing time in the evening. These men looked a bit like what I'd call "ruffians". Like rough biker types. They went to look at a 55 T-Bird we had. I didn't recognize Charlie at first. He had a bandana on his head, and wore a black leather jacket, blue jeans and biker boots. And sported some facial hair growth. I did not immediately warm to these men. I was a bit stand-offish. After a few minutes of looking over the car, they approached me to ask some questions. It was then that I recognized Charlie Sheen. I almost choked on my soda.

I got my composure and managed to answer their questions, and gave Charlie the keys to the car so they can start it up and examine it more. After a short time, Charlie gave me back the keys, they thanked me and left. Wow, I thought. I judged the book by the cover and was wrong! That was Charlie Sheen! Cool. Both men were nice and polite.

ROBERT URICH: Dec 19, 1946 to April 16, 2002. Age 55.

Dec 1989, Mid 90's, and 2000's. I first met this ruggedly handsome man in Dec 1989 at Hermosa Beach, Calif. He was filming the tv movie "Blind Faith". I asked a nearby production assistant if I could have a photo with him. She said she would ask as soon as they were finished shooting. My friend and I were at the beach that day to take photos of me surfing. While we waited for the photo op, I was very nervous. I fiddled with the settings on the camera that I barrowed from a friend. She had set the camera, and I messed it up. I shouldn't of messed with it. My chance came to have a photo with Mr.Urich. I stood next to him and my friend took the picture. He was super nice and joked around with us.

Later on, after the film was developed, the picture didn't come out good. It was too dark. Bummer. I wrote to him and received a signed photo that I still have to this day. From now on, I use a Susan proof camera!! Also called a "idiot proof" camera!. In the mid 90's with the advent and boom of the internet, I was able to join the largest Robert Urich fan club online. RUFriends on Yahoo Groups.

I made several really good friends of which we continue to stay in touch. When we learned that Robert had cancer, we all pulled together. Robert had made his own website so that we can get correct facts and information about his health and life. He became a member of our families. We poured our love out to him, and he gave back. More than he ever needed to. He was so down to earth and caring. On several occasions he expressed appreciation to us for our support of him and his family as they went through his illness. This lead to many public appearances he made. He would speak about his cancer experience and inspire us all.

When we met him, we felt the need to give him a big hug and assure him he will be fine. He will survive. We gave him all the love and support and spirit we could muster. Through these many public appearances and events around the country, many of us were able to meet him in person. And give him a hug. I was one of these people. As a matter of fact, I may be the fan that had met him the most. As talked about on his website when he was with us. At one event in Florida, a golf putting event, he gave me and a friend each a golf ball with his name on it.

We were wearing t-shirts from his cancer foundation. He reached in his pants pocket and pulled out these golf balls and handed them to us. We were excited and thanked him for the gift. We took photos, golf putted and had fun that day. After the putting he gave a warm speech about fighting cancer. From time to time he and his wife and family would chat online with us. We all did our best to be there and save as much of the chat sessions we could. Robert Urich gave us, his fans, so much of himself during his illness. And even before he fell ill. He was always very nice and friendly with his fans. And generous. As many of his fans would tell us on the net, the experiences they had with him. He went above and beyond the usual call of duty for a celebrity. We will always love and appreciate him and never forget him.

His favorite flower was lilac. I am planning a memorial garden on my 5 acres in Florida to include friends, family and pets. And Robert. His space will be planted with a marker and his favorite flowers, lilacs. And perhaps a golf ball. Robert Urich was a prolific actor, best known for his role as Dan Tanna in the 70's tv series "Vegas", and as Spenser in the 80's tv series "Spenser For Hire". He holds the record for the most tv movies and mini-series. He was a wonderful family man, friend, actor, and man. He will always be remembered for his kindness and generosity.

KEVIN BACON: The 6-degrees man. And wonderful actor. I met him when I was a volunteer at a celebrity fundraiser event in L.A. During the early 90's. He was kind and friendly, and posed for a picture with me. I thank him again for his time and photo. During that event I met other celebrities as well. And saw a chair with Mel Gibson's name on it. Bummer that he wasn't there. I met Danny Glover, Kareem Abdul-Jabbar, and a few radio personalities.

BIG HOLLYWOOD PREMIERE

Only once in my life did I have a chance to go to a real Hollywood Movie Premiere. It was for the movie "Predator 2" several years ago. I got the ticket from a friend, of a friend that worked for a Big Hollywood Agent and could not attend. It was a last minute call and I dressed as quickly as possible and rushed to the Agency office. While I was waiting at will call for the two tickets, alone, a young man my age came to the window to give mail to the worker there. He saw that I was getting two tickets and we talked for a bit. I told him that I was alone and had this extra ticket. As it happened, he was just getting off work and went to the premiere with me. I think his name was Mike. It's been so long I can't remember exactly.

So Mike and I drove to the Westwood Theatres in my 1978 Datsun 280zx. Cool little sports car. We had a parking pass for the garage and promptly found a space. As we walked toward the theatre we noticed a red carpet coming from the entrance to the garage, running up and into the theatre. The way the red carpet lay was in a "T", with one end at the street side where the stars, directors and producers would exit their limos, and the other end at the garage where Mike and I came out.

Both meeting in the middle and heading straight down, passing rows of photographers and into the theatre. The same kind of theatre where us regular folks go when there is no Big Hollywood Premiere going on. It was really cool and exciting. I tried to be as casual as possible, while butterflies where going spaztic inside my stomach. I got to the "T" and began my walk past the photographers. Which none of them took my picture because I'm not a celebrity! I bet they were wondering who this funny looking girl is and how did she get in here? But nobody said anything and we gave our tickets and found a seat.

I got buttery and salty popcorn and a diet pepsi like I always do. Mike got some candy and a soda and we made ourselves comfortable. Now, one thing about movie premieres is that obviously they aren't going to show advertisements (or trailers as they call them) for other movies. This is their own movie and night to shine. And I also noticed that the sound was set REAL HIGH!! I thought I would go deaf. Everyone obviously turned off their pagers and cell phones and respected the quiet of the theatre during the movie. I sat with movie stars, directors, producers, and many people in the business. Most of them were wearing black as that seems to be the required color of clothing in Hollywood. Black, goes with everything. They all smelled good and looked good and were really nice.

Before the movie started I saw actor Gary Busy. And when a free moment came I went up to him and introduced myself and shook hands with him. He was nice and said "Nice to meet you Susan Miller". Not knowing who I was or why I was there. He now knew my name and that's all. He didn't question me. I'm sure he just figured I was there with someone important. After all, the public is NOT ALLOWED to these Big Hollywood Premieres. It's strictly "their" territory. The people in the business and the actors and filmmakers. You show respect when you are on their turf. I also noticed that I was probably the only one in the entire theatre that was munching down on fattening, sloppy, buttery, yummy popcorn. After the movie was over, everyone clapped a lot. And then nobody was quick to leave. They all sat there watching the credits of course.

And would clap enthusiastically when their names came up and the names of their fellows. By each department. Editors would clap. Grips would clap. Art dept and props would clap. Stunts would clap. Music and so on. I thought it was kinda funny. I would sit there and clap too. Even though I didn't know anybody. What the hell. When in Rome. When the very last credit rolled people got up and began to leave. I held back as much as possible while trying not to get in anyone's way. I wanted to see if I can meet any other actors. There was a upper level in this theatre and I think a lot of the big ones where up there.

I stayed as long as I could then drove Mike back to the Agency office. That was so fun. I was so nervous walking down that red carpet. I saw exactly from the point of view that movie stars see. I was aware that I didn't want to be in anyone's way. Can you imagine? Brad Pitt walking down the red carpet and there's me, fat little goofball standing in his way!!? Ummm, excuse me miss but I need to get around you. Thank you. Who is she?? What's she doing here?? Hee hee. Umm, excuse me, I'm just passing through. Nice cameras you got there. Some of them are awfully big!! Hee hee. Can I get you some popcorn Mr.Pitt?

ROY ROGERS & HIS WIFE DALE EVANS. 1970's.

I have a scar on my left big toe from Roy Rogers. My Stepmother took my younger brother and I to the local movie theater to meet Roy Rogers and his wife Dale Evans. We were standing in a crowd around them, when Roy backed up, and I was underfoot, and he accidentally stepped on my foot with his big cowboy boots. I yelled loudly, and he turned around quickly and said "I'm so sorry, are you ok?" "I'm very sorry". My toe was bleeding by I would be ok, and have a little scar as a souvenir. My stepmother got a autograph, and we left the theater and went home.

CHAPTER 8
WRITERS & THE WRITING LIFE

I've always been a writer….in my mind. Constantly running stories after stories over in my mind. I called it "Self-Entertaining". When I was in my early 20's I started writing them down and completed my first screenplay. I have always been a big daydreamer. Mind wandering. Trying to complete a full fledged novel is a fun challenge. My process goes like this: Get it all down, no matter how sloppy or error filled. Then go back and edit and fine tune it. However long it takes until the finished product is ready for public reading. This approach to writing is similar, I found, to how I have done many other things in my life. Like music. I would break the piece down into small parts, memorize them, and then put it all together. This was back in High School when I was a drummer.

And Karate. We have these things called "Katas" or "Forms". A series of movements in a pattern of punches, kicks, and blocks. The way I tackle a large task is to break it down into smaller sections, memorize them, and put it all together. It will be very sloppy at first. My instructor would see me out on the mat and come flying out of his office in a fit. He was worried that I would be learning bad habits. This drove him all but crazy watching me. I tried to assure him and explain to him what my process was, and he wouldn't hear of it.

So I would endure his wrath, going through the motions, until he was satisfied and went back into his office. He wanted every punch, kick and block to be perfect. Not sloppy. I was trying to memorize the pattern of the kata. Then go back and fine tune it. There was no way I would let my punches, kicks, and blocks to stay sloppy. I was and still am, smarter and better than that. But he didn't realize that. So after he went into his office, I would pack up my things and leave. I would go down to the beach and practice my kata there.

Breaking down the pattern into smaller sections, learn each one, then put it all together. By the time my instructor saw me next, it was obvious that I had been practicing on my own. And in class, when he would ask if I wanted to stay afterwards and work on the kata, I would decline, stating I had a second job to do. Which most of the time I did. But the main reason was that I did not want to work with him, his way. On my own time. During class was one thing. 1 hour of training. We both were after the same end result: A perfect kata. One that would pass any and all tests forthcoming. We just had two different ways of achieving the same end result. I see this in my writing as well. First drafts are usually hideous.

But I let myself go and not worry about it. Because I know that I will do my fine tuning later on. Producing a perfect, or as perfect as it can be, end result. I like to share all this with you if you are interested in writing. Writing anything. Novels, screenplays, short stories, etc.. I feel, it doesn't have to be perfect right from the start, and may actually hamper you're progress. My writing life is spent trying to get as much of my work done as I can, when I have the time. As of this writing, I am a long haul truck driver and do not have the ideal writing environment. Like my own room and writing desk.

I am currently working to own a home in the next 4 years. That is my goal. So for now, I must live and work in this Big Rig with sleeper cab, drive the freight relocation tour, and payoff my mortgage on my bare piece of land. I don't feel that my current home life is ideal for writing, but I have to work with what I got. And this means putting my new laptop on my steering wheel, using the wheel like a desk, and write when I have the time and am not too tired from driving all day. I mean to have progress no matter what. To get things done, instead of waiting for a better place to do my writing.

FAVORITE AUTHORS
I would like to share with you some of my favorite authors. Being a long haul truck driver, I get to listen to a lot of audio books. And I read too. Actual paperback books. Seeing the words in print. Feeling the book in my hands. Looking at the writing style. I am a story first, author second kind of person. I will read the cover and if I'm interested in the story, I'll buy the book. That simple. I like anything to do with writers and writing. If a protagonist in a novel is a writer, I'll buy the book. I want to hang around. Watch and listen in this writer's life. See them squirrel away manuscripts in a safety deposit box. See them have drinks in a New York City bar with their editors. Deal with their publishers, go to book signings, and more. I have a list of my favorite authors so far.

Let's start with STEPHEN KING.
It took me a long while to warm up to Stephen King. It's because he scared the living crap out of me. And I know this may sound strange, but I mean that as a compliment. It was his tv show "IT". That horrible, scary, wicked clown. It scared me so much, that I avoided Stephen King for years. With the exception of "The Stand". I did watch that on tv and was intrigued by it. I love that "what if" situation. I enjoyed the movie, and later, the novel as well. It wasn't until he wrote "On Writing, A Memoir of the Craft" that I began to get into his work. And his book "On Writing, A Memoir of the Craft" was interesting to me as a writer. I wanted to hear his point of view on the art, craft, and job of writing.

I enjoyed that book on audio tape over and over. Wearing out the cassettes. Listening to his voice narrating his book. So, from that point on ("On Writing") I'm an avid admirer of our "Uncle Stevie" and his stories. I found that not all he writes is scary, or horrific. Many of his stories are heartwarming. Two examples I can give you is "The Shawshank Redemption", and "The Green Mile". It feels good to have a writer of his caliber among us.

Some of my other favorite authors are: Peter Straub, John Grisham, J.K. Rowling, Carl Hiassen, Randy Wayne White, singer/writer Jimmy Buffett, Janet Evanovich, Sandra Brown, Ernest Hemingway, James Swain, Robert B Parker of the Spenser and Jesse Stone novels. I will always have a soft spot in my heart for Spenser, thanks to actor Robert Urich that played Spenser in the 80's tv series. Lawrence Sanders, Max Allen Collins of the tv show CSI books, and Elmore Leonard. To name only a few.

AUDIOBOOKS: I am picky about the readers of audio books. One reader I cannot stand to listen to is: DICK HILL. He sounds like he's a bad actor that couldn't get a job acting, so he takes up reading audio books. Mainly for Brilliance Audio. I don't like how he makes the characters sound.

Either too stupid, too much like a dumb redneck, or he imitates Al Pacino mob style speech, or he imitates Actor Sean Penn in "Fast Times at Ridgemont High" the surfer dude. Sean made that character fun. And it's acceptable when the young man is a surfer. But some of these "accents" are highly abused by poor performers/readers. They must think the listener wants a "dazzling performance". No, we don't. We want a good, straight, entertaining, and not insulting to the listener, reading. Some readers I like are: Ron Mclarty, Jason Culp, David Colacci, Author Stephen King, Actor Willem Defoe (reading Stephen King's "Secret Window, Secret Garden"). Also, Frank Muller, Barry Bostwick, Tony Roberts, Jim Dale that reads the Harry Potter series, Anna Fields, and Boyd Gaines to name just a few.

There is one lady reader that I found annoying. She read for Janet Evanovich's book "Metro Girl". If you can get past the "Dingy Broad" sound that the reader projects, you will enjoy the story. And she makes the male lead sound too much like a dumb redneck. What is it with some of these readers??? Making the characters sound really dumb? Even if the characters are not that smart, most people do not talk like that. This is laziness on the part of the reader, as far as I'm concerned. And I wonder what the author had in mind for how the characters sound and act. They usually write some description in the story to paint a picture for us. But....some readers are just too hard to listen to. I can't usually make it through the first cd or tape. Some readers seem like they should be reading for children. Like Dick Hill. He would be better off not reading Randy Wayne White and others' novels', but reading to children instead. But, I think, he may just insult the children's intelligence as well.

OVER 50 STORY IDEAS

Yes, I have them. Tucked away in my safety deposit box. I'm open to wheeling and dealing with anyone with the right intentions and credentials. Perhaps we can sit down and talk about a partnership of some kind. I write down and save every idea I have. All my stories and ideas have been copyrighted as well. Just the usual protocol.

CHAPTER 9
BUSINESS IDEAS MAKING MONEY
Two for You and Me

1) DOGGYWOOD. Dog amusement park. Obstacle courses, sandy beaches & swimming pools for dogs & owners together, games, challenges, free run & play area, food, drinks, snacks, souvenirs all for dog & owner. Picnic benches, restrooms, shady clean facility. Charge a small admission price, have photo ops, dress ups, shows, etc.. The name, trademark, and copyright of "Doggywood" are held by myself and my company.

2) AIR SURFING. Using cables to pull you through a water track. Safety cables hold you up, and you can grab onto a handle, like wake boarding. Go straight, hit curves and banks, catch some air. Flexible cable allows maximum movement and maneuverability.

These are just two of many business ideas I have. I would like to meet with potential business people and form a partnership with them. I would get a small percentage of profits in payment for my idea services. All my ideas are always copyrighted and documented. The usual protocols.

CHAPTER 10
THE YEARS THAT MATTER   Essay.
Includes: Treading Through Molasses * Death Dream * The Crying Man * Letter From
A Drug Abuser

THE YEARS THAT MATTER.   Essay.

We have been given life. So, we make the best of it. We enjoy the things in life that we can.
We also carry too much emotional baggage that we can all cleanse ourselves of. Why carry it?
Why do that to yourself? I know it's easier said than done. But I feel we should, that is, if we
are not already, toughen ourselves up to the fears that have an influence on our lives. May I
suggsta starter? Write a long letter, by hand, ink & paper, to the family member, parents,
spouse, child, friend, co-worker, boss, or whatever. The people that cause you the most frief
in your life. And send it to them. Tell them how you feel, honestly. Tell them how much
they hurt you. Stand up to them in the letter.

Tell them how much of a pain-in-the-ass they are to you. And how you don't need to hear
all that crap from them all the time. They annot control you. This is the most emotional
baggage we carry. Do you agree? Of course, wouldn't life be so much nicer without all the
fear and bullshit we have to put up with from each other? I feel, there is so much insecurity
in so many of us out there, that we've bread a nation of control freaks. Driven by power and
fear. Fear to stand up for yourself against the dominating forces in your/our lives. We can,
and have, handed this fear and insecurity down to our children. It's like an American
tradition. We spend so much of our adult lives drugging ourselves, drinking too much
alcohol, hiding behind religion, drugs, cigarettes, and drink, to get away from it all. We are
supposed to be the land of the brave.

But how brave are we, really? In our daily lives? Do you feel, like myself and many others
I've spoken to, that's IT'S ALL AROUND US. Only the strong survive. Drugs, alcohol,
smoking cigarettes, machismo, is a sign of weakness? The users admit it. It's sad, isn't it? We
have been poisoning our people for centuries. So many good lives, wasted because of the
fear that drives them. Now, of course, what if the subject(s), of your letter will not read it?
Well, you have made a STAND. Against them. Against the depression and opression "They"
put you through. By writing and sending that letter. "They" may react in anger. They're
control over you is slipping through their hands and they can't handle it. Thee isn't a whole
lot we can do with some of the family we are stuck with. Except write the lette, tell how you
feel, change your address and phone number, and stay away from them.

You may even have to change jobs as well. If "They" treat you badly, obviously "They" do
not deserve you. And believe me, you are NOT ALONE. Dump that weight and live free.
Cleanse yourself. Go to a peaceful, quiet place and meditate. THINK. Clear your head. Make
time for yourself. Don't let "Them" push you into doing drugs, smoking cigarettes, or
abusing alcohol. They have NO POWER over you. And they will move on to a easier target.
Stand up to them. Don't hide behind anything. We should be proud to be smart, not live in
weakness.

We should all pride ourselves on doing the best and smartest things in life that we can. We all have the same opportunities to live better, and do better. By living a good, clean life, that in itself is Rebellion and strength. Don't' let "Them" break you. They will try. But hold your ground. And build your personal Army of friends and family that stand behind you and back you all the way. We should take pride in supporting each other physically and emotionally. By physically, I mean actually being there. In person. You let your Army know that you are going into "combat" or confrontation, and they can be by your side during the painful event. I don't believe that this support is a sign of weakness at all. It's a show of strength and unity. After all, do we expect our military to go into combat alone? One soldier, by himself, one gun.

Go get em' boy. We'll just wait here for you? No, that soldier is not alone, he's surrounded by his fellows, all fighting for the same cause. Same as in life and facing our own personal conflicts. Why in the hell should we have to face it all alone? Who's stupid idea was that? Call your friends, get them to come over, and witness the exchange. There is strength in numbers. It doesn't mean you need people to hold your hand during tough times, but support you physically and emotionally. And , you can hold hands if you want.

After all, many things in life are hard and painful. It's comforting to have that help and companionship, and caring for each other on that level. It's not weak. It's smart and strong. Soldiers hold each other when the going gets tough. They break down and cry. What they are going through is horrible. There is no shame in crying on your fellows shoulder. Thankfully we all have those support people in our lives, and in our military. Fellow soldiers, fellow Americans. These are the years that matter. In your life. LIVE FREE.

TREADING THROUGH MOLASSAS

Do you realize we can spend our entire adult lives in financial debt/ We don't need to live like that. Do you agree? Plan on financial control and freedom. For many of us, life feels as though we are stuck waist deep in molasses. Just slowly slogging through. I felt like that for most of my life. Until the day I stared living in my ugly old van. The "molasses" was all the weight I was carrying on my shoulders. In my heart and mind. Wanting to live my own life, my own way, free. Free from religious control and guilt trips. Free from societies attitudes and beliefs that we all must live on certain way or be condemned. Live "Their" way. Like good little puppets. Step out of line and lose your foot. DO WHAT WE SAY, NOT WHAT WE DO.

The control freaks all around us. Life doesn't work that way. Especially in a free country. I was always stubborn and hard headed. I knew eventually I would get out of this slog, and be more free. I racked my brains every day trying to figure it out. To solve the puzzle. I felt trapped and enslaved by the standards and attitudes our world has become. One example is home ownership. The prices so high it seems out of reach so why try for it? I am luckier than my female predecessors. I have more opportunity than they had. How can I get out of this trap I feel I am in? They say you have to live a certain way. I had to un-learn everything I was taught and reject everything people were telling me. Trying to get me to follow their way. To some degree, yes, of course. Get a roof over your head, clothes on your back and food in your stomach. The basic survival needs.

But to sacrifice my sanity and freedom to pay rent? Something I didn't have any control over. Living and working with people that drove me up the wall every day? Making rude and insulting comments each day? This is "Their" idea of how life should be lived on some level. It was misery for me. I couldn't stand it. Put up with all that just so I can be stuck here and pay rent like a good little trapped puppet? After the new apartment owners raised the rent too high, I had to move out. And into the van I went. The prevailing attitude among everyone in my life circle was that you were expected to live in a nice, upper class, expensive home.

Anything else was just trash and low class. Unacceptable. Even living in a apartment was considered low class. And a mobile home trailer meant ridicule. White trailer park trash for sure. Even though you can actually be a clean, intelligent, hard working, non drug and alcohol abuser, decent person. If you lived in a trailer, you were trailer trash. It's still that attitude today. Although improving somewhat. Many trailer dwellers are banding together into co-ops and buying the land on which their home sits on, in the park. So that it's not sold out from under them and they have to re-locate.

Many older folks on a fixed income live in these such parks. Nice, clean, decent people. And just because you are stuck in a low wage job, and all you can afford is to live in a trailer, in my opinion does not make a person trailer trash. Whatever their circumstances, this may be the best they can do. And some people may live their to save a bundle of money. For retirement, home buying, or what have you. Many Americans have been guilty of making fun of trailer park dwellers. Which, in my opinion, lowers the guilty to a level lower than anyone, anywhere. To boost their egos' at someone else's expense. Does not show class or intelligence, in my opinion. Many of us Americans have been raised with this fear of living that way, and fear of ridicule.

Many have been raised to make fun of those in trailer parks. Laugh and call them trash. Sure, there are people that are trashy, but not just in trailer parks. Have you done much looking around you lately? Trash is a way of life and a attitude and can befall any normal American. No matter where you live. Many of us are programmed to think fellow Americans to be bums, living certain ways. Like in a van or in a trailer park. But in reality, there can and have been many clean and decent, hard working people living that way for reasons of their own. Living in the van for me was one of the best things that could of happened to me. It may sounds strange.

I had a epiphany while living in the van. Not only did living that way cleanse my heart and spirit, and bank account. I didn't have to worry about rent or noisy neighbors anymore, but I also realized that I didn't really need much in life. Just a bed, a bathroom, and a shelter. This experience allowed me to dump all the emotional and mental baggage I had been weighed down with. It unlocked the door that I had been banging my head against for years. I learned one of my life's greatest lessons in that van. Just my boxer dog Brandy and me, and my books and music. I had all that I needed. And peace and quiet as well. The stress had been lifted. I would drive down to the beach, Manhattan & Hermosa beach, and park near the water.

Walking my dog on the strand and going for a surf or swim when the weather was warm enough. It felt great. Helped me to cleanse my life. I parked and would watch the ocean, looking for pods of dolphin, and enjoy the view. While expensive condos' sat near me. I got the view for free. I would sit their and chuckle a bit. I was free from the molasses that had bound me for years. It opened up more thinking for me. And I began down a new path in my life and have been all the better for it. Less stress, more emotionally and mentally healthier. And with not paying rent, I could afford to eat too! At least more than one skimpy meal a day.

I felt that I had climbed and scratched my way out of the molasses pit and onto flat, safe ground. I lay there, exhausted, excited, exuberated. I cried. I was free now. I can think more clearly. Better. Start making plans and changes. Stress lifted. It only took 30 years to get there!

DEATH DREAM

During a particular stressful time in my life, I had the scariest dream I've ever had. An Out-Of-Body-Experience. In the dream, I was perched up in the ceiling, in the corner, in a hospital. The doctors were frantically working on me. Trying to save my life. I was young. I don't know what cataclysmic event brought me to the hospital, but there I lay. In real bad shape. I looked up and to my right and saw a white light, like a tunnel, getting bigger as it drew closer to me. I looked back down at myself on the table. The doctors had stopped working on me. And they called it. Time of death. And I remember thinking "Well, I guess this is it". And I felt a *calm* coming over me. Like nothing I've ever felt before. I wasn't scared. My life didn't flash before my eyes. Then I looked up at the white lighted tunnel and put both arms out to dive in it, and went to it.

Then I woke up. Sweating and breathing a bit funny. Spooked. That was the first and only time I ever *felt* a dream. It stayed with me. It will always stay with me. From that dream onward, I was conscious about being extra careful. Walking across the street, driving, and life in general.

THE CRYING MAN. One of my favorite things to do in my spare time is to go to a bookstore. I browse. I read. I buy. On one of these trips I was browsing a self-help section. Looking for something about finances and investing. This section was near the self-improvement, relationship, health and others area. I was reading through a book when a handsome man came over into my section. He began looking through the relationship books. Now, I am the kind of person that is often overlooked by most people. I'm low key. Dress casual tomboy. Not your usual better dressed and better looking type people.

Quite possibly the least person you would suspect. This man looked as though he had just walked out of a GQ magazine. Short brown hair, clean shaven, nice slacks and shirt. Nice expensive looking watch. Nice shoes. And pleasant cologne. He looks like the kind of man that pulled into the parking lot in his late model Mercedes. Although he looked handsome and attractive, his face looked sad and troubled. He looked over to me and asked me a question. I did my best to give him an honest answer. He looked on the verge of crying. Then began telling me about his wife and family troubles.

He was expected to live a certain way by his family and his heart was aching. He was torn between what they wanted and expected of him, and what his heart truly felt. There were problems with his wife, something she had done. I tried to give him comforting and encouraging words. I was just looking for something on finances and suddenly I become a counselor. The further he got in his story, the more he looked like he was going to cry. He reached the point where he couldn't hold back anymore and began to weep. I reached over and placed a caring hand on his shoulder. I thought to myself, "Here I am, some lazily dressed tomboy, and here is this wealthy looking handsome man and he chose me to talk to". I felt honored and surprised.

I reached out to him with compassion the best that I could. To this stranger. He cried a little while longer and then thanked me for my kind words and time. We shook hands and he said he would buy the book he was holding. He found some answers in that book that would help him. I surely hoped so. And we parted ways. It was quite a unique experience. And I'm glad to have helped him in my small way. This handsome stranger. This crying man.

LETTER FROM A DRUG ABUSER:
I don't care about you. I hear you say you love me, but I don't love you. I want to love you, but I'm afraid. I don't want to feel. I'm too afraid, gripped by fear. I don't love or care about myself. Maybe I will be dead soon. Then I can rest. Found this letter on the sidewalk on Hollywood Boulevard.

CHAPTER 11
MOMENTS IN YOUTH

HALLOWEEN HORRORS. Every Halloween at our local elementary school they would hold Halloween festivities. Like haunted house, bobbing for apples, costume contests, games, prizes, dunking booths, candy, food and drinks. I was 5 years old the first time my family took me to Sepulveda Elementary School Halloween Festival. The chosen costume for me this year was a cute little bunny rabbit. Complete with white fuzzy tail. The evening was going fine, no problems. Kids running all over the place. A good size crowd. Our family has many children. Some boys and some girls. One of my older brothers was trying to scare me about going into the haunted house. He said that boogey men were going to jump out and grab me.

He laughed as he said it. He thought it would be really funny if I got scared enough to cry. He was your typical 9 year old boy. When it came my turn to go into the haunted house, my dad went with me. I was too young to go alone. Everything went fine at first. I was determined not to be scared. I wasn't going to let my big brother laugh and get the best of me. I was going to show him. I mentally prepared myself for the boogey men. Ready and waiting for them to jump out and grab me. At the beginning the house seemed pretty tame. Even for a 5 year old. Until the vampire. My dad and I were almost finished and were walking the last stretch.

Suddenly, a vampire jumped part way out of his casket to scare me. I was ready and waiting. I hauled off and punched the vampire square in the nose as hard as I could. The teenager playing the vampire let out a surprised scream. And then yelled "Hey, what the heck did you do that for?". His nose was bleeding. Actual real blood. My dad was so surprised and embarrassed, he apologized profusely to the vampire. We came out of the haunted house with not the looks on our faces that my brother was expecting. Dad looked mad and I was smiling. I thought it was funny punching that vampire in the nose. My dad reached over and whacked my brother on the head. Saying it was his fault trying to scare me like that. "She went off and punched the vampire" he yelled. That night, I was the cutest little bunny rabbit with a right cross.

LITTLE SISTER'S REVENGE. Never, and I mean never, pick on your little sister while on a long car trip. My two oldest brothers thought it would be a fun way to pass the time. Pulling my hair. Touching me. Blowing air in my ears. We kept fighting back and forth like kids do. Pushing me. Shoving. Back and forth. Mile after mile. Parents yelling that they will pull over the van if we don't stop it. I was sitting on the end closest to the door. I felt sick. I told my parents. They said try to wait until they can stop safely. I couldn't wait. So I let loose all over my bratty brothers. Ha Ha. And that's for picking on me. Take that you pigs. They were covered from head to toe in my vomit. In their hair, eyes, ears. On their clothes. In their laps. On their cool basketball shoes. All over them. Ha Ha. I laughed so hard. They were not happy campers at all.

FISH STORY. My big brother loves fishing. He was about 12 at the time, and I was about 8. We were out camping one summer like we always do. There was a lake near our campground and my brother and I went fishing. I didn't catch anything except hooks in my fingers most of the time. I had to have my brother bait my hook for me. I was too clumsy. He, on the other hand knew what he was doing and caught a fish that day. A good size perch I think it was. Every fish my brother caught was a big proud prize for him. This particular warm summer day, he decided to let me carry the prized fish. Wow. What an honor.

My big brother letting me carry his fish. I was excited. I took the fish from him, my brother having placed the chain through it's gill and mouth, in order to carry it. We walked slowly back to the camp. About a mile away. Lost in our own thoughts and daydreams. My brother walked ahead of me all the way there. We didn't talk much. Just strolled along. I dragged the fish on the ground the whole way back to camp. Over rocks, dirt, cactus, and asphalt. Walking and daydreaming. Dragging the fish. I actually thought that the fish scales were like it's suit of armor. Like I saw on the cartoons.

We got back to camp and my brother said "Hey Susan, show Dad the fish I caught". So I held up the mangled remains of the prize fish. Barely any flesh left. Eyes gone. Bones showing. Tail half torn off. My brother's eyes got as big as quarters. He was shocked. He started yelling at me. Loud yelling. He was really upset. I started crying. He yelling, me crying and my Dad just stood there dumbfounded. He finally managed to calm us down and we went off to supper. There would be no fresh fish for dinner that night.

A few months later we were camping again. My brother went off to go fishing. My Dad said that I should go with him. I shook my head sadly, kicking the dirt with my tennis shoes and said "No, he doesn't want me around. Not after what I did to his last fish". My Dad persisted so I ran to catch up with him. I told my brother that Dad wanted me to come with him. He gave an acknowledging nod and we walked on to the little pond. A short while later he caught a big catfish. He pulled it in and hooked it to the chain and then handed it to me.

My brother said kindly "Here, you can tell Mom and Dad that you caught this one". I let out a huge smile and took the fish and said "Wow, thanks David". We walked back to the camp and I held that catfish as high as I could. We made it back to the camp with one good, un-molested catfish and big smiles on our dirty little faces. Thanks again David, for that fish.

BRATTY LITTLE SIS. One of my older sisters was in our bedroom preparing for a date later on in the evening. She squeezed herself into pants two sizes too small as was the style of the 70's. I told her if she wanted that she could wear my pants. They were at least four sizes too small for her. She told me to go outside and play and stop pestering her. I watched as she piled on makeup to try and be sexy. Telling her that she missed a spot here and there.

When she finally finished getting all dolled up, she sat in the front room waiting for her date. Like most teen girls do. Me, on the other hand, being the bratty little sister had other plans. Her young man came calling. My parents met him, interrogated him for awhile then waved goodbye as they walked out the door and to his motorcycle. I waved goodbye too, and called after my sister "Bye, have a good time, don't get pregnant!!".

THE CANDY BAR. 1970's Halloween. As most kids do, our family of misfits dressed up in various costumes and hit the streets. Looking to bag as much candy as we could in one night. Besides the usual fruit and candy, was a particular prized candy bar. The fictional name I give this candy bar is Big M. This type of candy bar was rare to get. It was big and expensive. You were definitely the big winner if you scored a Big M. You beat everyone. Since I was one of the younger kids, I had to come home earlier than my older siblings. Per my parent's rules. I sat in the living room of our house and counted my evening's loot. I did not score a Big M. I was disappointed a little.

Just then one of my older sister's came in the house. She had a big bag full of goodies. She dumped the bag near me and sorted through her candy. She found what she was looking for. SHE got a Big M. Wow, cool. I got all excited about it. This sister of mine was and still is a sweet, wonderful and kind sister. She began to load her candy back into her bag and leave the bag on her bed, grab another pillow case and head out for some more. This was typical of pre-teens in that day in age. I couldn't get that Big M out of my little pea brain.

She asked me if I would watch it for her while she was out. To make sure none of our brothers would take it. Wow. Me. A big honor. Yes, of course I will be happy to watch your Big M while you are out. I'll keep it right here. In my lap. I'll protect it until you get back. She said fine and went out the door. I waited for her. And waited. I ate some of my candy. The Big M safely sitting in my lap, hidden by my bag. It seemed to take her a very long time to get back. For a 10yr old kid a half hour seems like forever. I waited. I did not want to let my sister down. I didn't want to disappoint her. My mouth was drooling over this candy bar. It was a big, rare prize. I looked at it. And looked again. I waited. And waited a little longer.

This candy bar tempting me. Never have I been that tempted in my young life. The Big M was calling to me. I tried hard to resist. When is my sister coming back? She better get here soon. I looked at the candy bar again. Temptation. Waiting. All that waiting. I couldn't hardly stand it any longer. I looked down at the Big M sitting in my lap. I ate it. I popped the last bite in my mouth, feeling the overwhelming guilt. I would make it up to her. I'll buy, or steal her 10 new Big M's. She would understand. She came home. "Where is my Big M that I asked you to guard for me?" she asked. I just looked up at her and didn't need to say a word. She knew. She yelled. "You ate it! How could you?". I was so sorry I started to cry.

I apologized. She was fuming mad. I had betrayed her. Let her down. She would never trust me again. It took her a little while, but she eventually forgave me. Things were back to normal. Talking nice to me like she usually does. Also, maybe it helped when I *acquired* about 10 replacement Big M's for her. I really wanted to make it up to her. All is well. And we'll never forget this Candy Bar Incident.

POKER NIGHT AT THE MILLER'S. Every once in awhile my parents would invite a few of their friends over to our house to have drinks and play poker. This particular evening they gathered in the living room and quickly got under way. Laughing and having fun. Drinking and playing. I was told to go to bed and stay there.

Do not come out of my room. There is a reason kids don't listen to their parents. Because kids are curious and more exciting things are going on outside of their bedrooms. I snuck out to have a peek. They quickly caught me and I ran back to my room. Laughing and thinking that this little game is funny. Now, let me tell you a little bit about one of my older sisters'. She loves acting and Broadway. We had to share a room and I had to listen to her music weather I liked it or not. As a teenager, over and over again she would play the same Broadway musicals. A Chorus Line, My Fair Lady, and many more. I wound up memorizing these musicals. So then I decided that it would be fun to sing them.

I went back out into the living room where my parents were drinking and playing poker with their friends. All laughing and having a good time. I jump in and start singing "Kids! What's the matter with these kids todayyyyy!" And on and on I went. Singing and dancing. My own little Broadway show. My parents' were embarrassed and their friends thought I was cute. One of them said to my Dad "Hey Joe, I didn't know you were going to have live entertainment here tonight". My Dad escorted me back to my room and practically tied me to my bed so I would stay there. Gave me a peck on the cheek, turned off the lights, and closed the door. I was only good for one show. Any more would be too much. I fell fast asleep, with Broadway musicals dancing in my head.

BURNT LOG. Our family went camping every summer when we were kids. On this particular trip, we had a little problem at the supper table. Feeding a family of 9 including 7 kids can be a hectic chore. As our mother prepared our meal, she wrapped corn on the cob in aluminum foil and put them in the open fire to cook. When they were blackened and finished cooking she took metal tongs and pulled each one from the fire, and put them in her cookpot. She then gave each of us kids a corn, still wrapped in it's foil.

Placing it next to the other food on our paper plates. One of my sisters' poked at hers with her fork. She exclaimed "Hey, this isn't a corn, it's a burnt log!" Our Mom told her that it was a corn and stop fussing and eat it. My sister continued to protest. "It's a burnt log!" It was when the log began burning a hole in her paper plate and the table cloth did Mom realize that my sister wasn't kidding. She quickly grabbed the burning log with her tongs and threw it back into the fire. Then rummaged around in the fire until she found the foil wrapped corn and gave it to my sister. We all ate our supper with our usual gusto and my sister got to enjoy her corn on the cob.

QUEEN OF SKATEBOARD HILL: One of my favorite sports as a kid was skateboarding. I was a major tomboy. By 1976 I was 12 years old and got my first skateboard. This was before they insisted on safety pads and helmets. This first board I wore out completely in a few months.

It had metal wheels with ball bearings to ensure a smooth ride. I would race around a corner going so fast that sparks would fly from my metal wheels. I would also lose most of my ball bearings. It got to the point where I would be on my knees collecting them and carry a tool with me to take off the wheels and replace the bearings. Re-install the wheels and go tearing down the hill again and again. Shortly after I destroyed my first skateboard, I got my second one. This time the manufactures thought they had built better wheels. These were Flintstone type clay wheels. Like the stone age! I would be skating down the sidewalk in front of our house at full speed and hit a bump in the concrete.

Usually where tree roots cracked and raised a portion of the sidewalk. I hit this crack so hard I was instantly airborne. I must of flown 20' and crash landed on the concrete. I got up, bleeding from new wounds and opening old ones. I looked at my board and noticed a large chunk of the wheel had broken off. I still skated anyway. Until there were too many chunks missing and I couldn't go ka-lunk, ka-lunk down the sidewalk anymore.

So there went that board in the trash. They finally came out with urethane rubber "Cadillac" wheels that are still used today. The urethane I mean. Now I was back in action and ready to expand my skating area. The biggest challenge in our South Bay-Torrance, Ca neighborhood was Huge Hill. The biggest, meanest, knarliest hill around, a couple miles anyway. If you rode your skateboard to the bottom of the hill without falling, you were the best skater and bravest in the neighborhood. Major bragging rights. Our biggest challenge. On one sunny summer day, a group of about 10 neighborhood skater kids gathered at "The Hill". Might as well call it Hamburger Hill because that is what you will look like if you fall off your skateboard. The big event was on. One by one they faced their fears, put on their bravest 10,11,12,13yr old faces and down they went.

Speed wobbling into one spectacular crash after the other. This hill was so long, steep and bad that nobody was able to make it all the way down to the bottom. They crashed or bailed before they reached the halfway mark. At the bottom of this hill was a dead end street. Then it was my turn. I took a big gulp of what felt like rocks in my throat. I was sweating with nerves and fear. The kids all gathered around me. Teasing and taunting. Calling me that worst of all childhood words: "chicken". Or wimp. None of us had any safety gear on. No knee or elbow pads. No gloves or helmets. It just wasn't worn back then. The kids kept egging me on.

I took a deep breath and set my skateboard on the ground. Slowly, I mounted it. Right foot forward, goofy foot stance. With my tiny rapidly beating heart in my throat, I kicked off with my left foot. I gained speed so fast. Quicker than any other time in my young, 12 year old life. I bent down to hold onto the front with my right hand, and grabbed the rear of the board with my left hand. Trying to keep my weight centered on the board. The inevitable speed wobbles began before I could even reach the halfway mark. The farther down the hill I went, the faster I would pick up speed. The speed wobbles got worse and worse.

Harder and harder to keep my hold on the board. It didn't help that my hands were sweating profusely. I lowered my center of gravity as much as I could. Squatting down like a baseball catcher. I gripped the board tighter. I wasn't going to let go for anything. This board will have to buck me off. Faster, faster. It felt like I was up to 20 mph. Wobbles got bigger and faster. I held on for dear life and kept my eyes open the whole time. In a matter of seconds I passed the midpoint. I was already farther down than the other kids, will I make it all the way to the bottom? The wind howled in my ears so loud that I couldn't hear the kids yelling. My eyes were as wide as they could get. As big as quarters. 20mph, 25,30mph...and ...
CRASH!! The speed wobbles finally threw me like I knew it would. My board catapulted my little body about 20' and slammed me hard on the asphalt. I rolled over and over for what seemed like five minutes. Sliding and grinding my knees, back, head, arms, elbows, every inch of me.

Thrown and slammed hard like a rag doll. I finally came to rest in the gutter. At the bottom of the hill. My head was ringing from a slight concussion. My vision a little watery and blurred. I couldn't see or hear the kids running down the hill to congratulate me. A nearby concerned adult that had been washing his car, and witnessing us crazy kids, ran over to see if I was ok. He took one look at my bloody, battered body and insisted I go to the hospital. This was before the advent of 911. I managed to get to my shaky feet and told him I was fine. Wiping blood from a head wound out of my watery eyes. Not to worry about the especially bloody mess that was my right arm.

I slid on this arm for about five feet before flipping over and sliding on other parts of my body. Don't worry about the pieces of skin hanging down and tiny rocks of asphalt embedded in my wound. The kids all gathered around me, yelling with excitement, pride and astonishment. They clapped me on the back and I winced in pain. I was trying to smile and be cool. I was almost too sore to revel in my victory. Standing there, a little wobbly, dripping with blood. I grimaced a smile back at my friends. That day I was Queen of Skateboard Hill, and I was the coolest and most respected skater in the neighborhood. Yes, but at a bloody price. No pain, no victory.

Years later I went back to look at that hill. Remember as a kid, everything seemed so big and impossible? I stood at the top of this hill and looked down. It's still a big, steep, and seemingly impossible hill. As I stood there, a couple of boys on skateboards rode up to me. I asked them if they ever skated down this hill. They looked at me and replied "Hell no. What are you, crazy?". And they rode off. I laughed.

THRASHER KID: I went through bicycles at an alarming rate as a kid. This had my folks worried that there was something seriously wrong with me. Nothing at all was wrong with me, I was just a stunt kid. I would take my new bike out to our dirt place and ride bmx. Bicycle Moto Cross. The neighborhood kids and I built jumps, berms, and ramps. A virtual race course. One summer day, a big kid named Billy decided he was going to trick me. We were racing our bikes around the course when I hit the biggest ramp as fast as I could. To get as high in the air as possible and fly the farthest. While I was in the air, about 15' or so, Billy rolled a car tire right into my landing path. I landed on the upright tire and bounced off of it. Flying another 20' or so into the air and crash landed in a heap in the dirt.

I got up, nose bleeding, missing some teeth and looked at Billy. I told him, through spitting blood and dirt out of my mouth, that I was going to get my big brother to kick his ass. I took my shattered bike back home and got my brother. When we got there, all the kids where gone. My dad was not too happy that I had broken my new bike. I had to go several months before I got a new bike for my birthday. Once again, I headed for the bmx track and did my usual racing around. I didn't have any more problems with Billy that summer as he was nowhere to be found. Riding my new bike over the jumps I landed the wrong way. I landed on my front tire and bent the rim and broke the forks that held the tire. My dad again was mad at me. I didn't get another bike until Christmas. This was another Monkey Ward bike made overseas.

The other kids had Schwinn bikes. Stronger and better and made in USA. I was happy to get a bike no matter what kind it was. This time, I went to the dirt place and played with the other kids. One boy named Johnny was doing something really cool with his bike and I wanted to do that too. I was a stunt kid. Excited to try anything. At the far corner of our dirt place was a gas station. And behind the gas station was a almost vertical drop of concrete about 30 feet high ending at our dirt place. Johnny would start at the top and ride straight down, nose first and bang bang land at the bottom staying upright and riding away. The trick was to put all your weight as far back as you could. With your butt almost rubbing against your rear tire. Johnny would take his Schwinn, built strong and tough, down this drop over and over again.

Bang bang, real fast, bang bang his tires would hit. He made it without crashing every time. He was also smaller than the rest of us. This was such a big stunt that not all the kids would try it. They "chickened" out. Not me. No way. I didn't have enough sense to see that this could be dangerous and I could get hurt. Oh no. I was excited that this was a cool stunt and I wanted to do it. So I rode my cheap little Monkey Ward bike to the top and looked down. Wow, that is steep.

I could seriously do a fatal face plant right at the bottom. I'd break my neck and my parents would kill me. Yeah, how exciting. The rush of it. Just looking down and feeling the fear in my bones. In my blood rushing through my little body. I mounted my bike, looked straight down again, and off the lip I went. No turning back now. Gripping the handlebars as tight as I could with my butt hanging back as far as I could, I hit bottom. Pulling up on the front wheel just before I hit the ground. BANG BANG. Both tires hit real fast. I made it. Yeah! Cool! I jumped up and down with excitement.

It was only Johnny and I, or me and Johnny as we would say back then, that where the only two that could make it. I wanted to go again. So up to the top I went. Looking down at the drop, I let myself fall. BANG went my front tire. The back one flipped me over and the bike threw me into the ground. Once again I was eating big globs of dirt. But always coming up with a smile on my dirty, bloody face. I didn't make it that time but wasn't hurt or worried about it. When I picked my bike up to go again, I noticed that I cracked the frame. Where the joint of the steering met the main frame. I now had two pieces of bicycle to carry home. My dad just looked at me with this angry, astonished, and confused look on his face. "What's the matter with you?" he bellowed. I heard that line a lot when I was a kid. I was worse than all four of my brothers combined. "That's the third bike you broke!!" my dad yelled. "That's it!! You're not getting another bike ever again. And don't go asking or begging for one. I've never known anyone to destroy bicycles that bad and that often. What are you? Getting hit by cars or something?". He yelled. "From now on, if you want a bike you're going to have to build one yourself". He said. And so I did.

With the help of one of my big brothers. I got really good at building bikes. And when I got older, I moved from racing bmx at Ascot Park in Gardena, to racing motorcycles. I was always a stunt kid. I would actually crash on purpose because I thought it was fun. And that way, when I crashed in a race, it didn't scare me. I actually liked crashing!

I was a thrasher kid. Thrasher being the name young people gave to explain acts of destroying or crashing ourselves or our equipment. Skateboards, bikes, dirt bikes, cars, whatever. If you smashed it, you were a thrasher. Or better yet, in Southern California, you were a Thrasher Dude, or Thrasher Chick.

BURNT MARSHMALLOWS: As you know, my family did a lot of camping when we were kids. One of our favorite things to do at night was have a campfire and toast marshmallows and have s'mores. The first time I ever tried toasting a marshmallow I was about 5 or 6. It fell off my stick and landed in the fire. I cried for a new one. They gave me a new one. I lost that one too. They told me I better not lose this next one. I pushed it deep onto my stick and held it over the fire. It caught on fire and burned black to a crisp. I threw it away. My parents gave me another one and told me that if I burned this next one I had to eat it. I thought they were kidding. They weren't. I burned the next one to a black, charred crisp. I cried trying to get out of having to eat it.

They insisted. So, slowly I took a bite. Then more. Then ate the whole thing. I actually liked it. My family thought I was weird. I was. And still am. While their marshmallows were lightly toasted brown, I burnt mine to the black, charred crisp and happily gobbled them up. Ha ha. I still eat them that way today. I love to shock people with that. It's funny. Here, have a burnt marshmallow on me. Enjoy!

BEAR ATTACK: One summer as our family was camping at King's Canyon Park in California, we had a bear encounter. I was about 10 when this happened and my two older sisters' were about 15. My teenage brothers would customarily sleep outside under the stars. One night after we had dinner over an open fire, cleaned up, washed dishes and went to bed, we had a big, furry unwelcome visitor. Our family had a huge tent that we had put up and inside we had bunk bed cots to sleep on. In the middle of the night we awoke to the sound of my brothers yelling and trying to open the tent as fast as they could. "Hurry, hurry!" they yelled excitedly. They made it inside as we were waking up.

Then I felt something pushing me from the outside. I was in the top bunk above my sister Linda. I felt another shove so hard that it pushed me out of my bed onto the floor. I was fully awake now and screaming for my dad and my sister. The dog was barking hysterically and my brothers were yelling. "A bear!! Dad, a bear!!" Screams and chaos filled our tent. The girls were yelling, my Dad was yelling, the dog barking non-stop. My dad was angry at having been so rudely awakened. He grabbed the flashlight and opened the tent. Intending to scare the damn bear away. When he opened the tent, there was the bear, all 7' of him, standing in the doorway. Dad screamed, dog barked, kids screaming, Dad shining the flashlight in it's face, and the bear just had this look on his face like this place is crazy and he turned and ran away. As fast as his furry bear butt could move.

Never, and I mean never, wake the Miller's in the middle of the night unless you want hell to pay!! The bear had torn up the wooden food cabinets that were the standard in the 70's at campgrounds. And he decided that he would follow my brothers into the tent to see what else he could eat in there. He was in for a big surprise. Good thing that bear got away before my dad could get ahold of him. I was jumping with excitement. "It pushed me out of my bed!" I exclaimed. Soon after, no doubt waking the entire campground with our hysterics, we eventually all went back to bed.

SNAKE UNDER BED: When I was young, one of my brothers liked snakes a lot. He would easily catch them whenever we went camping. And sometimes he would sneak them home. On one such trip home from camping, one of his snakes got loose in the camper while we were driving. The snake slithered across the floor and us girls screamed and jumped up on the table. We didn't know it at first, but this was just a harmless garter snake. But to a girl, a snake is a snake and we were hysterical.

My Dad pulled over to the side of the road and we all jumped out. After my dad smacked my brother in the head for bringing a snake in the camper, we got the snake out and let it go in the woods. We all piled back into the camper and went on our way. Well, my brother never had just one snake. He didn't tell anyone that he had several more. I found this out later on when we got home. I promised not to tell. And I didn't. Until now. One night when the entire nine member Miller family was fast asleep, I felt a movement under my bed. We had a 4 bedroom house with hardwood floors. My two sisters' and I shared one room. And 3 boys in another room. The baby brother had his own room next to my parent's room. I felt the movement get stronger and stronger. I jumped up and sat on my knees in my bed and looked around.

I thought for sure it was the dreaded boogey man. No. It wasn't. There was something under my bed, making it move across the room. I screamed as loud as I could for my sister to wake up. "Linda! Linda! Linda! There's a snake under my bed! I screamed. The bed still moved around the room on the hardwood floor. I yelled some more. Linda woke up and asked what the heck I was screaming at. My bed stopped moving. I told her that a snake had moved my bed, actually, our beds, all around the room. She looked around at the re-arranged furniture trying to figure out what had happened. Then my parents entered our room and asked if we were ok.

They saw that our beds had moved all over the room. I told them that a snake moved them. I was about 7 or 8 at the time. They said no, it wasn't a snake. It was a earthquake. The Landers Quake several miles to the north of our Torrance, Calif home. You know it's bad when your parents come in to check on you. They put our beds right and told us to calm down and go back to bed. I couldn't sleep. The aftershocks kept me awake and shaking in my bed. My sister comforted me. My other sister practically slept through the whole thing. She didn't say much during this whole ordeal. The next day we drove up a little north to check on my cousin Stephen's home. They were closer to the quake's epicenter than us.

Their home had big cracks in the walls. I couldn't believe it. And along the drive we saw fallen bridges, power poles, big holes in the ground, and hillsides that crumbled. This was my first big earthquake. And there would be many more as long as I lived in Southern California. I have been in so many quakes, that I could actually tell you the magnitude. And when I would watch the tv news people in Hollywood, they would shake with a aftershock. And I would wait a few minutes for it to travel 30 miles south of Hollywood, and then I'd go stand in the doorway and here it comes. Rumble, rumble, shake, shimmy. The aftershock would hit us. Being in a earthquake is highly unnerving.

By the time I hit my mid-20's my nerves were so shot, that if I was in a building and it moved slightly, I would tense and hold my breath. One time I was in downtown L.A. when a trembler hit. I spent the night in a hotel room with a friend and his partner from work. We were all decent, no funny stuff. The men were handsome and slept in their tighty whiteys. At 3am it hit and I told them to get in a doorway. So there I was, in a glass hotel building, room, in a doorway sandwiched between two men in their underwear. I could imagine how this would look if we were found this way.

What would my family think?? The building we were in was newly built and down in the parking garage you could see huge round 10' thick rubber bumper support things in the building's structure. Those were shock absorbers. The building would sway in a earthquake like rubber. A stiffer building tends to crumble. This was the idea behind these rubber shock absorbers. I am living proof that these things work. The building swayed alright. And swayed, and swayed, and swayed. Seemed like for 10 minutes we were going. Then the aftershocks hit and we were back in the doorway swaying to the earthquake.

This partner of my friend had never visited California before. This was his first time. So naturally we take him to the usual tourist spots; Hollywood, Studios, Beverly Hills, The beaches, surfing, L.A. Riot area, driving on the freeways dodging bullets, and of course, for the full California experience, we throw in a earthquake in a glass hotel building so he can have his *full* monies worth. He said he's never coming back to California again. Oh well. We will miss him. But, that's ok. We will always have plenty of fresh, I mean, new visitors.

THE HALLWAY INCIDENT: When I was a teenager I would go out driving with my friends. We would pack as many teens in my friend Phillip's car as we could. I was never the late night kind of person so when it reached about 9pm, I was already starting to get tired. By the time my friend dropped me off at home, I was ready for bed. Just worn out from getting up early, going to school all day, then band practice, then chores, then hanging out with hyper, chatty teens blasting loud music into the later hours of the evening. I came home on this particular night, grunted "hi" to my parents as I walked past them, sitting on the couch watching tv. I was walking down the hallway to my bedroom when all of a sudden the bedroom door raised up. I stared up unbelievingly at it.

What happened? The door just raised up! Well, I didn't hear or feel anything. But my parents heard a big crashing sound and came running into the hallway. Seems I fell into the floor heater. I looked down and saw that my right leg had been swallowed up as far as my hips, and my left leg was laying bent and flat on the carpet. I looked like a karate person standing on one leg with the other leg up and bent and ready to knock a round-house kick into you. My parents started to laugh. I started laughing too.

The heater, thankfully, was not on so it did not burn my leg. As it turned out, my mom took the grille cover off the heater to clean and repaint it. My parents pulled me out of the hole, and with a red, embarrassed face, I went on to bed. The next day they were on the phone telling everyone that "Susan fell into the heater!".

FIRST TIME DRUNK: I was about 22 years old the first time I got drunk. I was a bit of a nerd when I was younger and was too afraid to go to parties. Too shy. But this time I decided that I was missing out on an experience and I must go to this party. My friends' helped convince me to go. We got there pretty early, probably about 9pm. I was a wallflower and sat in the corner drinking a soda. After awhile I figured, what the heck, I'll just try one beer. Just to see what it's like. I watched as everyone was drinking, talking, dancing and having a good time. There must have been about 30 people there that night. This was a big house in a middle class neighborhood in Torrance. As the night wore on, I had more drinks.

I remember shots of tequila, and I can't remember all the other stuff I drank. My friends' were playing drinking games and we were all getting pretty smashed. My speech slurred, I wobbled as I walked. Everything sounded like I was in a dream. Wow, it was pretty cool. And fun. And I felt so rubber like and relaxed. And I laughed a lot. At everything, and nothing. And the music played loud, and there were people dancing and I wanted to dance too. This was the 80's and break dancing was the craze. I thought I would just show all these party goers that I could do break dancing. I got down on the floor and started something that looked a little like breaking, then seemed to evolve into something like a fish out of water. Then it looked as though I was having some sort of weird convulsions, flopping around, here and there. I was yelling and laughing and flopping around to the music. Rolling all over the floor. When the song stopped I looked around and everyone in the room had left. I was the only one there.

So, I got up, brushed carpet fuzz off of me and went into the next room where all the people went. Had some more drinks, and started dancing again. Another break dance song came on and down I went. Rolling all over the floor, thinking I'm just so cool and hip, and flashy. Flopping like a fish, looking really stupid. The song stopped and I looked around. Everybody left again. I was alone. Ok, I could take a hint. They don't like my break dancing. Heck, I was probably going to knock a few of them over and hurt somebody, or hurt myself. So I just stumbled over to a bench in a hallway and sat there and buzzed. Smiling and laughing and watching the people. Look at all those people. There are so many.

And, who's this? Johnny. And his girl. Oh, that Johnny is so hot. He's a gorgeous hunk. Did somebody say that he owns this house? I think so. Johnny and his girl. His beautiful, model like girlfriend are standing right in front of me. I'm also looking for pink elephants and don't see any yet. I'm sure I will see them though. I've heard all about those pink elephants. I reach over and grab a piece of Johnny's ass. I laugh. Ha ha. Hi Johnny, how's it hanging? He and his girl both turn around at the same time and just look at me. I think, "Oh shit, I'm going to get punched". So I just sit there, swaying with my drunkenness, and wait for the punch. It doesn't come. They just look at me with mixed sympathy and amusement then walk away.

Later on in the wee hours of the morning, my friends' find me passed out on the front lawn. They wake me up and say I can't sleep here, this is a nice neighborhood. Full of us college people and working folks. They half drag me into their car and take me home. They put me on my bed like I am a wet noodle. Take my shoes, socks, and sweater off and lay me down to sleep. What good friends' they are. Next morning I am surprisingly fine. No hangover. They can't believe it. Me either. They are sick and feel like they've been ran over by a Mack Truck. We lay around all day nursing each other and resting. They tell me there is another party, next weekend. "Hey", they ask me, "are you going"?

FIRE EXTINGUISHER (High School): My friend had a big fire extinguisher that held about 5 gallons of water and also had a nozzle to fill it up with air. We would build the air and water pressure as high as it would go, then take it with us when we went out driving. Usually around Halloween. We would pick on the older kids, like junior high teens. We'd see them walking the streets in their Halloween costumes and stick the nozzle out the window and give them a good soaking. Laughing, we would drive away fast. Sometimes we would drive up to a fast food place and place a fake order. When we would get to the window, we gave them a gush of water instead of money. Laughing hard and racing away.

One Friday night after a football game, we went out cruising. Packing as many teens in this old car as we could. I was in the front seat on someone's lap and I was in charge of the fire extinguisher. We spotted some high school teens hanging out by their cars. I said, "Let's spray them". My friends agreed and we got close enough to spray. Across two lanes of traffic, I let loose with the hose just as they were turning around to look at us. Drenching them solid. Oh shit! It's the quarterback on our football team and some of the players and some girls. The players jumped in their fast trans-am cars and chased after us. We had no chance of outrunning them in a cheap ass Vega. My friend being the crazy stunt driver he was, saved all our necks.

He swerved down one street. Players right behind us in fast pursuit. My friend ran stop signs, stop lights, turned right, left, and raced down streets. With the football players hot on our tail. They knew who we were too. We were band twinkies. That's what they called us if we were in the marching band. My friend played sax, and I played drums. We were going to get thrashed by these guys if they caught us. Quickly, my friend screeched around a corner on a residential street, and turned into a dark driveway. No lights were on at this house. We hoped nobody was home.

Everyone in the car layed down on each other as flat as we could make ourselves. He turned his car lights off and we sat quiet. Waiting. Then we heard them. Racing past us. Two trans am cars, with big, fast engines. All souped up too. We waited a little while longer until we thought it was safe to move. Finally we got up, turned on the car, backed out of the driveway, and sped home. Oh we were laughing so hard. Until Monday. Back at school, here come the huge, tall, burley football players. One of them grabbed my drumsticks and broke them in two. Another guy shoved my friend.

We threatened to call the cops if they hurt us and they would go to jail. No football career for you boys, we'd see to that. After threatening and cussing at us for awhile, they let us go. Whew! We survived that one. From then on we just stuck to junior high kids and fast food places.

SWITZERLAND '79' When I was in High School, our band went to Switzerland the summer between my freshman and sophomore years. It was great. 2 weeks and 3 days. That was the best summer I've had. First, I won a all expenses paid trip to Maui, Hawaii for one week. Then, four days later I left for Switzerland. I was 14. In the band, I was a drummer. Playing tri-toms. Three drums bolted together and attached to a harness. That thing was heavy but fun to play. I marched in the Rose Parade with those drums too. Now, you take over 200 high school teens, assorted adult chaperones, our band director and fly them all to a foreign country for a summer tour, and you have organized chaos. They bussed us all around the country. It was great. We saw Geneva, and all the major cities, and even some small villages. We stayed in hotels, youth hostels, and even a bomb shelter. When you have American teens in a foreign country, not used to the food, problems can arise. Take the bread rolls for instance. We were all seated in this huge cafeteria eating our lunch.

They gave us these rock hard bread rolls. Imagine, 200 teens taking knives and stabbing their bread rolls. Banging them on the table. Throwing them at each other. Using the rock hard bread as a weapon to knock someone unconscious. Bang, bang, bang. We pounded and stabbed at our bread rolls. We did not know what to make of them. At home, our bread is soft. Not rock hard. It didn't occur to us that you can dip the bread roll in milk to soften it up before eating it. We generally don't eat soggy bread in America. So we didn't wet our bread. Eventually, we gave up on it. We lay the semi-mutilated bread on our plates, after eating everything else that was familiar, and left the building.

I happened to notice the surprised looks on the faces of the workers at that cafeteria. All that pounding and banging and stabbing like crazed murderers. I'm sure they were glad to see us American teens leave. The rest of the trip went pretty smoothly. We didn't lose anyone, and nobody got shipped back for being really bad. We marched in the Fest De Geneva Parade (Swiss Independence Day). And had a lot of fun playing and sightseeing. My friends and I even rented a boat and I found a vase at the bottom of Lake Geneva. I gave it to my parents when I got home. It's a monumental undertaking to haul over 200 high school teens overseas. But our little West High School, Torrance, Ca band pulled it off. Prior to the trip, we were selling candy bars for months to raise money. Washing cars, doing every thing we could to raise the needed $2000 per student. It was a great trip. And I will never forget it.

THROW ME INTO THE WAVES: If you haven't noticed already, I was a weird kid. I grew up a mile from the pacific ocean in Torrance, Calif. Our family would make regular trips down to the beach. I loved these beach trips. I would be so excited, jumping up and down and all over the place. I even wore my bathing suit under my dress when we went to church. I couldn't wait for bible study to be over so I could go swimming. One of the first trips we made was when I was about 5 or 6. I remember that I had not learned to swim yet.

My parents wouldn't let me go out too far in the surf. This one particular early trip, my older brother and sister thought they would have a little fun with me. They literally picked me up and threw me into the waves. Knowing full well that I would wash up on the sand like a beached sea lion. I would wash up crying and wiping sand and salt water from my eyes. They would laugh and grab me and throw me into the waves again. I would cry every time. Standing up and pulling sea weed out of private places. Again they throw me. This time I was beginning to get used to it. I would relax and let the wave take me. I opened my eyes and it looked as though I was churning around in a washing machine. I would see a rock here and there, but mostly sandy bottom. They kept throwing me and laughing while they did it. It soon got to the point where I was "one" with the wave and was starting to like it.

So the next time I got spit up on shore, I asked them to throw me again. And again, and again. It didn't take long for the fun to run out for them. It's not going to be funny if I actually like being thrown into the waves. My brother finally called me weird and they walked away. I didn't leave. I waded out into the water and body surfed. But I wouldn't catch the wave like you're supposed to. I went "over the falls" as we call it. And crashed landed on the ocean floor. The waves were about 2' tall but big enough for a little kid like me. I was a runt. Over and over I went. Over the falls and flipping myself at the very last second so I would land on my back and churn around in the whitewash and be spit up on shore. I'm sure that this strange activity had the lifeguard a little worried. I imagine him thinking "What kind of kid actually likes wiping out on purpose?". A weird kid, that's who. A weird kid like me. My parents always had a hard time getting me to come out of the water and have lunch.

Finally, I did. Then went back in and played until it was time to go home. They had to drag me out of the water. Since then, I have not been afraid of the waves. My brother and sister actually did me a favor. I will always respect the ocean as it is very powerful and can do anything it wants to you. I took up surfing in my teens and still love the sport today. I had this 8' 2" Bing Surfboard that took both my friend Mike and I to carry. He in the front and me in the back, and switch from time to time. We would surf all day, every day in the summer. I wish I still had that board. In my heart and soul, I will always be a surfer. And I'll get out on the water every chance I get.

RIPTIDES

I would like to give you a word of advice when it comes to rip tides. Rips are small rivers that pull swimmers out to sea. People usually fight them, panic, lose energy and drown. They swim and swim and go nowhere. They don't realize it's like swimming in a river, up stream. If you ever find yourself in that situation, point yourself left or right, parallel to the shoreline and swim sideways out of the rip. Out of the little river, then back to shore with the tide. Don't panic. Just turn and swim parallel, along the shoreline and you'll get out of it. It's always a good idea to swim near lifeguards and have friends or family with you. Don't swim alone.

Chapter 12
RECIPES FOR YOU TO ENJOY

1) ENGLISH CHILI

INGREDIENTS:
- 3 pounds beef chuck
- 2 1/2 cups chopped onions
- 5 cloves garlic, minced
- 2 (14.5 ounce) cans stewed tomatoes
- 1 (15 ounce) can tomato sauce
- 1 (12 fluid ounce) can or bottle beer
- 5 tablespoons chili powder
- 1 tablespoon dried oregano
- 1 tablespoon paprika
- 2 tablespoons ground cumin
- 1 tablespoon brown sugar
- 4 tablespoons beef bouillon granules
- 2 bay leaves
- 1 tablespoon salt
- 1 teaspoon ground black pepper
- 2 (15 ounce) cans pinto beans, drained

DIRECTIONS:
Place meat in freezer until slightly frozen. Cut into 1/4 to 1/2 inch cubes.
In a large skillet over medium heat, brown meat until it turns gray. Stir in onions and garlic.
Cook until onions are tender, about 5 to 10 minutes.
Cut up canned tomatoes, reserving juice; combine in a 6 quart cooking pot with tomato sauce, beer, chili powder, oregano, paprika, cumin, brown sugar, beef base, bay leaves, salt, and pepper. Bring to a slow boil over high heat.

Add meat mixture, and reduce heat to low. Simmer, uncovered, for 2 to 3 hours. Mix in pinto beans. Simmer for 1/2 hour longer. Taste, and adjust seasonings if desired.

2) CHILI MAC SUPREME
This is an old family recipe. It's a wonderful, 'stick-to-the-ribs' meal that goes wonderful with warm cornbread or rolls.

INGREDIENTS:

- 1 cup elbow macaroni
- 1 pound ground beef
- 1 small onion, chopped
- 1 cup chopped celery
- 1/2 large green bell pepper, chopped
- 1 (15 ounce) can kidney beans, drained
- 2 (10.75 ounce) cans condensed tomato soup
- 2 (14.5 ounce) cans diced tomatoes
- 1/8 cup brown sugar
- salt and pepper to taste

DIRECTIONS:

Bring a pot of lightly salted water to a boil. Add pasta and cook for 8 to 10 minutes or until al dente; drain. In a small saucepan, simmer celery and green pepper with water to cover until tender; Drain. Place ground beef in a large heavy skillet over medium heat. Cook until evenly brown. Add onion, and cook until tender and translucent. Drain excess fat. Add celery and green pepper. Stir in kidney beans, condensed tomato soup, diced tomatoes and brown sugar. Season with salt and pepper, and stir in macaroni.

3) SPINACH DIP

Water chestnuts add a delightful twist to this chilled spinach dip. Serve with wheat crackers

INGREDIENTS:

- 1 (10 ounce) package frozen chopped spinach, thawed and drained
- 1 (16 ounce) container sour cream
- 1 cup mayonnaise
- 1 envelope dry vegetable soup mix
- 1 (8 ounce) can water chestnuts, drained and chopped
- 3 green onions, chopped

DIRECTIONS:

In a medium bowl, mix together spinach, sour cream, mayonnaise, dry vegetable soup mix, water chestnuts and green onions. Cover and chill in the refrigerator approximately 2 hours before serving.

4) ARTICHOKE DIP

Susan's Artichoke Dip

Parmesan cheese bubbles on the surface of this rich chafing-dish dipper that gets its tang from marinated artichokes. Three cloves of garlic punch up the flavor of this favorite appetizer.

I am always asked to make this dip for parties and family gatherings. It is always the first thing to go! Serve it with either crackers or breadsticks." Original recipe yield: 4 cups.

INGREDIENTS:

- 1 (10 ounce) package frozen chopped spinach - thawed, drained and squeezed dry
- 1 (14 ounce) can artichoke hearts, drained and chopped
- 3 cloves garlic, minced
- 1/2 cup mayonnaise
- 2 (8 ounce) packages cream cheese, softened
- 2 tablespoons lemon juice
- 1 cup grated Parmesan cheese

DIRECTIONS:

Preheat oven to 375 degrees F (190 degrees C). Lightly grease a 7x11 inch baking dish. In a medium bowl, mix together the cream cheese and mayonnaise until smooth. Mix in the artichoke hearts, spinach and Parmesan cheese. Season with garlic and lemon juice. Spread evenly into the prepared baking dish. Bake covered for 20 minutes. Remove the cover, and let the dish bake uncovered for 5 more minutes, or until the surface is lightly browned.

5) LINDA'S GARLIC CHICKEN forty garlic chicken

A simple soup of boiled chicken, vermouth and a boat load of garlic. Do not let that scare you, as its sharpness softens beautifully in the cooking. Be sure to serve with a loaf of good bread, as the baked garlic makes a delectable spread.

Tender boiled chicken AND a soft garlic spread for your bread! What a combo! You can also add carrots and onions to the chicken/garlic 'stew'. You'll get lots of praise, but no more vampires! Serve with slices of fresh sourdough bread, if desired." Original recipe yield: 4 servings. Throw in some lemon too.

INGREDIENTS:

- 1 (2 to 3 pound) whole chicken
- 3 1/2 cups sweet vermouth
- 3 medium heads unpeeled garlic
- 1 bunch fresh parsley, chopped
- 1 1/4 cups chicken stock

DIRECTIONS:

Bring a large pot of salted water to a boil. Put in chicken, boil until meat falls away at the bone. Pull out as many bones and as much skin as you like. Stir in the vermouth, garlic cloves (don't peel - you will use them for the bread), parsley and chicken stock. Reduce heat to low and let simmer and reduce for about 2 hours. Serve hot with slices of bread. Take the soft garlic and spread on fresh bread as 'garlic butter'. Yum!

6) JOHN'S LEMON- GARLIC PORK CHOPS

These flavorful chops are marinated overnight and then can be quickly grilled or broiled. The longer you steep pork chops in this lemon, garlicky, gingery marinade the more delectable the results. Then you can bake the chops with a sesame and bread crumb crust or you can omit the coating and go straight to the grill. Marinated for 2 hours these chops are very good, marinated all day they are exquisite. These can be done wonderfully on the bbq...just omit the crumb coating. Enjoy!" Original recipe yield: 4 servings.

INGREDIENTS:
- 4 thick cut pork chops
- 1 cup soy sauce
- 8 slices fresh ginger root
- 4 cloves garlic, sliced
- 1 teaspoon freshly ground black pepper
- 1 cup dried bread crumbs
- 2 tablespoons sesame seeds

DIRECTIONS:
Place pork chops, soy sauce, ginger, garlic, and black pepper into a large, re-sealable, plastic bag. Shake the bag gently to combine everything, and refrigerate for at least 2 hours. These are excellent done in the morning, and left to sit all day.

Heat oven to 350 degrees F (175 degrees C).

In a shallow dish, combine bread crumbs and sesame seeds. Remove chops from marinade, making sure there are no ginger slices clinging to the meat, and lay them in the crumb mixture to coat. If you like, place pieces of garlic from the marinade on the chops. Place chops on a rack or baking sheet. Bake for approximately 45 minutes, or until done.

7) URICH'S BACKYARD BURGERS (A Harley family special)
Throw in some seasoning and cook. In addition, here is a Aussie style burger too.

My Australian friend first made these burgers a few weeks after arriving in the USA. They became a hit with our family. They're a bit messy but delicious. Hunger busting burgers topped with every topping imaginable. Wrap your laughing gear around that. Crikey! It's a meal in one go.

INGREDIENTS:
- 1 pound ground beef
- 1 large onion, sliced
- 4 eggs
- 4 slices Canadian bacon
- 4 pineapple rings
- 4 slices Cheddar cheese
- 1 (8.25 ounce) can sliced beets, drained
- 4 slices tomato
- 4 lettuce leaves
- ketchup (optional)
- yellow mustard (optional)
- dill pickle relish (optional)
- mayonnaise (optional)
- 4 Kaiser rolls, split

DIRECTIONS:
Preheat an outdoor grill for high heat. When the grill is ready, lightly oil the grilling surface. Form the ground beef into four patties, and grill for 5 minutes per side, or until cooked through. Meanwhile, melt butter in a large skillet over medium heat. Add onions, and fry until soft. Remove the onions from the skillet, and crack the eggs in the same skillet over medium heat. Cook until the yolks are solid, turning over once. Remove eggs, and set aside. Place the Canadian bacon in the same skillet, and fry until toasted. Remove the bacon, and turn the heat to high. Quickly fry the pineapple rings in the bacon drippings just until browned on each side.

To Assemble sandwiches: Set bottom of Kaiser roll on a plate, and top with burger, a slice of cheese, a slice of Canadian bacon, one fried egg, fried onions, a few slices of beet, a slice of pineapple, a slice of tomato, and a leaf of lettuce. Decorate the top bun with ketchup, mustard, relish and mayonnaise as desired. Place over the burger. Repeat with remaining burgers.

8) PAUL'S HOLLYWOOD DISH. Mediterranean Greek Salad

Hearty, robust, and delicious! All the stuff you dreamed about in a Greek salad - tomatoes, olives, feta cheese, cucumbers, and sun-dried tomatoes - all glistening from a splash of oil. This is a great salad to take to a barbeque. All ingredients are approximate, so add more or less of any ingredient depending on your own taste. Original recipe yield: 8 servings.

INGREDIENTS:
- 3 cucumbers, seeded and sliced
- 1 1/2 cups crumbled feta cheese
- 1 cup black olives, pitted and sliced
- 3 cups diced roma tomatoes
- 1/3 cup diced oil packed sun-dried tomatoes, drained, oil reserved
- 1/2 red onion, sliced

DIRECTIONS:
In a large salad bowl, toss together the cucumbers, feta cheese, olives, roma tomatoes, sun-dried tomatoes, 2 tablespoons reserved sun-dried tomato oil, and red onion. Chill until serving.

9) SOOZ AVACADO MUSHROOM SPREAD

Your favorite mushrooms sautéed in butter with rosemary, garlic, parsley, vegetable stock and whiskey. The whiskey is optional but really makes it good! Serve cold or warm. Great on a pita with avocado! If you are like me, you buy mushrooms with the greatest of intentions, but unfortunately, they sit in the fridge and get really...weird. This recipe is simple.

I made it up, being determined not to let my mushrooms get... weird. The best part is that it worked, and tastes great. Keeps well in the fridge up to 3 days. Original recipe yield: 4 to 6 servings.

INGREDIENTS:
- 2 tablespoons butter
- 1/2 teaspoon fresh rosemary
- 4 cloves garlic, minced
- 3 cups chopped fresh mushrooms
- 1/4 cup fresh parsley
- 3 tablespoons vegetable stock
- 1 teaspoon cornstarch
- 1 tablespoon Scotch whiskey

DIRECTIONS:
In a large skillet over medium heat, melt butter and sauté rosemary and garlic until tender. Stir in mushrooms and sauté until juices run. Add parsley and stir occasionally to prevent sticking. When mushrooms are tender, stir in stock and mix well before adding cornstarch. Cook for 1 to 2 minutes, then add whiskey and cook for 1 minute more.

10) JANETTE'S LASAGNE

Sure Sooz! Okay here we go: Boil lasagna pasta but not all the way since it will cook more when it is in the oven besides it is also easier to work with when it is not fully cooked. Once you got the pasta finished you can put that aside in some water then after a bit take it out and place it on something that you know it won't stick to so when your ready for the pasta you can grab it. Please note that this recipe can be switched up for vegetarians, also you can use ground turkey (in fact I like ground turkey better than ground beef has more flavor).

Okay, so in a pan fry up some onions, while they are cooking add some garlic you can either use fresh or use from a jar don't need too much. Once you got the onions really friendly add your ground meat after it cooks up drain it and put it aside. Now you want to cook up some more veggies use whatever you like, I like celery, squash, mushrooms. Once you have the veggies cooked up add your sauce. I usually use a big can of regular sauce, one can of tomato paste, and a can of stewed tomatoes. (one more thing: if you want, you can also cook up some Italian sausage it usually only needs about 3, split them so the rough skin opens then just fry the sausage not the skin it breaks up easier in the pan).

Once you have the sauce cooking really good add all your meats and veggies also add some black olives cut up in there but make sure to save some for when you are layering. Once your big pot of sauce is heating up and getting friendly with everything I like to add a dash of ricotta cheese, actually I add almost all of it and save a little for the layering. Make sure you add some spices to your sauce like black pepper, dash of salt, pinch of oregano, couple of basil leaves or use ground basil leaves. Get your Pyrex dish, on the bottom of the dish take some of the sauce and spread it evenly on the bottom (this will ensure that your lasagna does not stick to the bottom).

Now place lasagna pasta horizontal till Pyrex is covered then evenly distribute sauce, then cover the sauce with mozzarella cheese (shred approx a lb of mozzarella or buy it already shredded). Then take more lasagna noodles and this time place them in the opposite direction and then cover them with ricotta cheese, then cover again with sauce. Keep doing this until at the very end on top of the sauce, sprinkle more mozzarella and on top of that you can place pepperoni slices, and olives and sprinkle with parmesan cheese and any left over ricotta (it will look like a killer pizza on top).

Place in oven at 350 degrees, also if you have a lot left over you can make two batches. You will know when it is done because the cheese will be melting and you will see it bubbling up. Take it out of the oven and let it cool for a while. You will be amazed at how easy it will cut because you have alternated your noodles back and forth and that is why it will be easy to cut and serve and you should not have too bad a mess on the bottom of your Pyrex because of the sauce you put on the bottom. Enjoy!! Take care, Janette

Chapter 13
GHOST STORIES AND HAUNTINGS

1) GHOST MOOSE, Modesto, Calif 1970's.

Hi Everyone, I've got a little ghost story for you. This is true, I'm not making it up.
When I was a kid, my cousin Eddie and I went playing in the small wooded area near our
Grandparents house in Modesto, Calif. We were playing hide and seek when I came upon a
huge moose in the trees. I froze still. We stared at each other for awhile. I was afraid it would
attack and bite me. My parents had warned me of Bears and other big animals when we
would go camping up north. I slowly backed away and then began yelling for my cousin to
come and have a look at this huge moose. He was so big, he towered over me. I was not
mistaken, I knew a moose when I saw one.

I found Eddie and we went looking for the moose, but couldn't find it, or as I recall, any
tracks or evidence that it was actually there. Naturally I told my family and they all dismissed
me as a imaginative kid. My cousin believed me. He heard my yells. I was a little scared.
So, many years later I am reading a Paranormal Magazine and they have an article about
Ghost Moose, and that reminded me of my experience when I was a kid.

MOOSE IN MODESTO?? Not usually. They are usually found up north, way up north near
Canada and way northeast in Maine. But not in Central California?? Weird yes. But what else
can I say? I was a kid, and I know what I saw. And I also think that this was a pretty cool
experience. I can laugh about it now. But back then I really thought it was real. Now I know,
it must of been.....a ghost??!!

2) WHO'S SCRATCHING MY LEGS?? When I was young, I was visiting my
Grandparents York in Perris, Calif with my family. One night, I had to share a bed with my
stepmother. During the night as we lay asleep, I was awakened by the pain of something
clawing my shins on both legs. I thought it was my stepmother and her long toenails. I
kicked and moved around, and eventually the clawing stopped and I went back to sleep.
When I woke up in the morning, I thought I would see my legs all bloody and scratched up,
but there was no marks on my legs. I told my stepmother that she scratched me with her
toenails and she said she didn't.

Thinking about it later, this was not a feeling of just light scratching, it was more like my legs
were being clawed by a person with their hands and fingers. It was one of the weird
experiences of my childhood.

3) I DREAM OF FIRE!! At my Grandparents Miller house in Modesto, Calif, one night, I
lay asleep on a mattress on the living room floor. We had a lot of family crammed in their
modest house. I was about 10 yrs old or thereabouts, when this very real and vivid dream
came to me. I dreamt that I smelled fire and ran out of the house toward the smell. I ran
down the street and around the corner to find a house fully engulfed in fire, with the fire
dept there trying hard to put it out.

I smelled the smoke, saw all the lights of the fire trucks, saw the huge fire. I stood there and watched it for awhile, before a fireman told me to get back home. I ran home. When I woke up, I told my family that a house was on fire down the street and that I went out to see it. And they said there had not been a fire, that I was just dreaming. Later on that day when I was allowed to go out to play, I followed my dream path and went down the street, and around the corner and looked for the house that I was sure had been burnt to the ground. I did not see any burnt houses. I was amazed. I really thought I had been there, and that I saw that house burning down. One day I will try and do some research to see if in fact a house near my Grandparents, on Hilltop Lane, in Modesto, Calif did in fact burn down at some time in the past.

4) A GHOSTLY KISS. One night, while laying asleep in the sleeper berth of my semi truck, facing the inside wall. I was slightly awakened by the feeling of a man trying to kiss me. He put his tongue to open my lips, and I lay half asleep wondering if this is real or what?? I went ahead and let him kiss me and I kissed him back. It was a lovely kiss, a kiss that I have given some special men in my past. A nice, soft, passionate kiss. I kept my eyes closed for fear he would disappear if I opened them.

When the kiss was over, I slowly opened my eyes, and did not see anyone there. For this man to kiss me in this position, he was actually "in" the wall of my sleeper berth. Of all the ghostly encounters a person can have, this was by far not a bad one at all. And this ghost is welcome to visit me again anytime if he wants. Another sweet kiss awaits him.

5) I'M OUT OF MY BODY!!! About 10 years ago, while living in a 1940's era apartment on Pacific Coast Hwy in Redondo Beach, Calif, I had a out of body experience one night. I was under a lot of stress, on the verge of being evicted due to loss of job, wages, etc.. This night, as I lay in my bed, I had a very vivid dream that I actually "Felt". I don't know of any dreams that you actually feel them. I dreamt that I was in a Hospital Emergency Room and the doctors and nurses were trying franticly to save my life. I watched them from my vantage point high in the ceiling, in the corner. I looked up to my right and saw a bright white light, then I looked back down at myself. I wasn't scared, or in pain.

My life didn't flash before my eyes. The doctors called it. My time of death. I remember thinking "Well, I guess this is it", and I felt a CALM coming over me, like nothing I've ever felt before. I then turned to my right, looking into the white light, and went toward it. I woke up just at that point. This dream shook me up a bit. I was in a cold sweat. I lay there thinking "Wow, when is this going to happen? When am I going to die". From that night forward, I was more careful driving, crossing the street, in every aspect of my life. I knew "Where" I was going to die (A hospital emergency room), city, state, unknown, but I didn't know "what" catastrophic event happened to put me in the hospital fighting for my life…and losing.

Was it a car accident? Truck accident? (I'm a long haul truck driver, 18 wheeler), was it a heart attack?? I don't know. This experience is a rare and unique experience. Not everyone has this kind of Out of Body Experience. Why me? Was it the stress?? Was I not living my life correctly at the time? Whatever the reason, I keep this experience in the back of my mind, and it helped me to not be afraid of death, or dying. Perhaps that could have been the reason for this experience??

In my younger years, I was really afraid of dying. I had lost my mother when I was about 4 years old. I don't know why I had this experience, but I don't mind that it happened to me. I'm not too worried about it. I see it as a kind of "gift".

6) STOP FOLLOWING ME!!! When I was young, I would often times have a dream of someone following me, I was terrified. To the point of paralysis, utter fear, and cold sweats. After enduring many years of this terrifying dream, I knew I had to confront my fear. So one night, I mustered up the courage to face what was following me. I was nearly frozen with fear, but I forced myself to turn around and face it. As I turned to face the being that was following me, I caught a glimpse of it. I saw a women, in white, with brown hair, and she quickly floated upwards and dissipated into thin air.

She was gone. Who was this women? Was it my birth mother? Maybe she was just watching over me and didn't realize how scared I was? Maybe this was a lesson in courage that I needed to learn? I don't have the answers, only some ideas. Whatever the reason, I will never forget this experience. And I've never had a dream of anyone following or chasing me, ever since.

Chapter 14
TREASURE HUNTING IN FLORIDA

1) SIESTA KEY. Using my metal detector, I found a man's gold ring and gold necklace with a gold and diamond pendant. These items total value is $1200.00

2) KEY WEST. Snorkeling just off the main beach, using my prescription dive mask so I can see, I used my metal sand sifter and found a gold coin from the 1800's. It has been valued at $500.00

3) ST. AUGUSTINE. Using my metal detector in the sand, while my dog romps and plays in the surf, I found a Women's diamond ring. Pure silver with 1 large diamond in the center, and 4 small diamonds on each side, for a total of 9 diamonds. The estimated value of this ring is $2000.00

I enjoy treasure hunting on land and in water every chance I get. As a truck driver, covering the 48 states, I take my metal detector with me. I have been to ghost towns, and meteor craters, and gold mines. Treasure hunting is a very fun and profitable hobby.

Chapter 15
TEXAS HOLDEM POKER

I have been playing poker regularly for about 5 years. This is a fun game and I earn some
extra spending money playing poker. I enjoy tournaments and cash games. Poker is one way
that a skilled player can earn more money playing poker than they do in their regular job.
Books, videos, tv shows, magazines and websites. All are great training tools and places to
play and make friends. I have been to the World Series of Poker in 2006 and met World
Champion player Phil Helmuth, as well as celebrity poker players Actor Tobey McGuire, and
Jennifer Tilly and actor James Woods.

My first foray into poker was in the mid 90's at The Bicycle Club in Los Angeles, California.
I didn't have a lot of money to play, so would play occasionally. On one memorable evening,
I was in a limit holdem game, $1-2, and the other players around the table kept raising and
re-raising me. It was stressful and intimidating. I held my ground and when the cards played
out, I walked away with over $100 profit. I quickly took my winnings and left. The players all
grumbled at me leaving with my winnings. I told them that I wasn't going to allow them to
take it back from me. Too much raising and re-raising me.

Years later, I started playing again, but this time, on the internet. I do ok, but am working on
getting a lot better. I see the financial potential that poker can bring. People make more
money playing poker than with a regular low paying job. The time has never been better to
get into poker.

Author Bio. S.L.Miller
Susan Miller is a native of Southern California. She attended college in
Torrance, Calif. She lives in Florida with her dog, Rowan. The Story Digest is
her first book.

http://stores.lulu.com/soozrowan

www.authorslmiller.com